MORE LARRY HATTEBERG'S
KANSAS PEOPLE

To Don —
Some of the finest
people in the
world live in Kansas —
That include's you!

Best Wishes —
Larry Hatteberg
1995

Given to me
from Michelle as
45th birthday gift.
This is a wonderful
book, I really like
the Power of Love
by Randy & Suzy Starms
Just a powerful story

The Hatteberg family has grown since our last book. My daughter Sherry married the love of her life, Steve Hilger. We are proud to count him as a member of our extended family. From left to right: Susan Hatteberg, Judy Hatteberg (back), Sherry Hatteberg Hilger (front), and Steve Hilger.

If a man is lucky enough to have a family who believes in him, nothing else matters. I do. To them I dedicate this book.

MORE LARRY HATTEBERG'S
KANSAS PEOPLE

Featuring photos by Vada Snider and text by Suzanne Perez Tobias

Printed in the United States of America by
Mennonite Press, Inc., Newton, Kansas

ISBN 1-880652-37-4
Library of Congress Catalog Number: 94-061197

Designed by Susan Burdick
Edited by Chuck Potter

On the cover: Wayne Dunafon of Westmoreland
On the back cover: (clockwise from top left):
Bobby Vaught of Wichita, Charles Little Coyote
of Medicine Lodge, Henry Westfahl of Arlington,
Alberta Hubele of Gypsum, Grace Wu-Monnat of
Wichita, Velma Wallace of Wichita, Robert Watson
of Wichita.

Vada Snider
Photographer

Vada Snider was born July 24, 1958, in Edmonton, Alberta, Canada. Her photos in the first "Larry Hatteberg's Kansas People" took her to London. An exhibit of photos from the book was displayed at Harrods for seven weeks in the fall of 1992. Since then, the show has been exhibited in galleries across the United States.

Snider teaches photojournalism at Wichita State University and maintains an active schedule as a free-lance photographer. Her photos have won numerous state, regional and national awards.

In addition to her photography work, Snider is a writer and professional flutist. She has spent seven summers as music reporter/assistant editor for the Chautauquan Daily in Chautauqua, N.Y.

Her flute career has included regional and national performances with touring musical theater companies, the Kansas Arts Commission Touring Program, and the auditioned flute choir at National Flute Association conventions.

A graduate of Bethel College in North Newton, Kan., Snider holds a master's degree in communications from Wichita State University.

Years in Kansas: 28.

Suzanne Perez Tobias
Writer

Suzanne Perez Tobias was born Aug. 19, 1968, in Fayetteville, N.C., the daughter of Armando and Regine Perez. She attended North Carolina State University, where she received her bachelor's degree in English in 1990. Soon after graduation, Tobias moved to Kansas to work for The Wichita Eagle. At The Eagle, she has covered city government, military affairs and general-assignment news.

Tobias and her husband, Randy, who was born in Hays and raised in Wichita, love to watch Kansas thunderstorms, play with their golden retriever and visit any small-town cafe that serves pie. Tobias also enjoys spending time with her little sister, Portia Figures, whom she met through the Big Brothers & Sisters program in Wichita.

Years in Kansas: 4.

Table of Contents
75 Profiles of 85 Kansans

This book all love stories that I have ever read. (handwritten)

Foreword

The TV monitor flickers slightly, as if being disturbed from the blackness of its cold sleep. A sound of plastic hitting metal breaks the silence of the videotape editing room. A videocassette appears to be breakfast for a machine ravenous for input. The tape is drawn down the throat of the videotape player. Clicks, buzzes and pops pierce the solitude of the room as the tape winds its way to an electronic climax. Then, as if called by a higher power, the TV monitor showers the room with images and sound.

Like old friends who have come to visit, the TV images of the many "Hatteberg's People" segments flood my mind with memories. Good memories of good people.

For the past 20 years, the "Hatteberg's People" TV series has brought me in touch with Kansans throughout the state. I have heard their stories. They have touched me with their honesty. They have uplifted my spirit on those days when life seemed to perch all its weight on my shoulders. I have laughed with them and sometimes shed a tear as their stories tugged at my heart.

My goal has been to be a storyteller. To focus on people whose lives are classrooms for the rest of us. I want each story to have a message. A message that enriches, that uplifts, that educates or just makes us think about who we are. Television time is precious, so it's important for those of us in the business not to waste it with the trivial and sensational.

My belief is that those ordinary people living ordinary lives are a vast, untapped source of information. We sometimes ignore them because they seem so normal. *That* is their great power. Because they are like us, we listen. We share experiences through the medium of television and grow because

of it. Video storytelling lets viewers share the experience of life. The camera is a powerful writing tool that sees beyond its focus. It brings us to the closet of the mind and through its subtle nuances forces us to see past an image and into the window of the soul.

Fred Shook is a professor of broadcast journalism at Colorado State University. He is also a friend and colleague. In his writings about broadcast journalism, some 15 books on the subject, his words put the

role of the video storyteller in perspective. He writes:

"A millennium from now, when archaeologists sift through the rubble of this age, some stories will be more valuable than others in helping them understand who we were as a people, what problems we faced, how we addressed those problems, and how we tried to live. Will the most useful record of this time be the endless debates of political discourse and the muttering of journalists reading the written word off TelePrompTers, or insightful stories of life the

archaeologists can see for themselves about everyday men, women, and children in the natural environments? The answer seems obvious. After all, stories about ordinary people are the foundation of history, and much of what we know and remember of this century, from the Hindenberg disaster to the moon landing, the collapse of the Berlin Wall and Tiananmen Square, comes from stories told narratively through the moving images, sounds and everyday conversations and confrontations of life."

Fred Shook is correct. We learn from each other through experience, and the *people* story on television provides the best avenue for education. As I work with people, I am humbled by what I hear. I have people tell me things they have never told another living soul. I have people tell me stories

S N A P S H O T   B I O G R A P H Y

Larry Hatteberg was born June 30, 1944, in Winfield. He attended Emporia State University and Wichita State University, studying broadcast journalism and photography. He and his wife, Judy, were married June 6, 1965. Years in Kansas: 50.

that surprise their spouse. As our lives intertwine during the storytelling process, I find that I usually learn something about myself while I am listening to others tell me their stories.

Sometimes they just give me the courage to go on.

It is the work of skilled and talented photojournalists who make our "Hatteberg's People" stories come alive. Without them, I would simply be a writer of forgotten words. With them, the power of television storytelling is at its best, the sound and

images flowing together like a video tapestry. I am honored to work with these talented people. In recent years it has been photojournalists like Dennis Decker, Paul Beam, Doug Raines and Brad Nygaard whose stories you remember.

For this book, the stories came to print through the efforts of gifted writer Suzanne Perez Tobias. The wonderful photographs are the work of photojournalist Vada Snider. Their biographies appear in previous pages of this book. My thanks also to Susan Burdick and editor Chuck Potter, whose insight gave the book form and structure. A special thanks to Bill Handy of The Wichita Eagle for believing in and supporting this project.

My biggest fan lives in Winfield. My mother, Mary Hatteberg Powers, has been a gift to my life. Her perseverance through life's difficulties inspired me. Her love has sustained me. She has given me so much, I honor her now with a son's everlasting respect.

My father, Merle Hatteberg, died in 1981. It was he who demonstrated his humanity every day as owner of the Peerless Bakery in Winfield. He was a gentle man who saw "friends," not customers, come through his door. He taught me that people *always* come first. Not money, not fame, but simply being there when others need you. He was . . . and in my mind still is there for me.

A few years after my father died, my mother married a wonderful man who has been a "gift" to the Hatteberg family. He is Bill Powers, a man who has given himself to the Winfield community. His support of quality education at Southwestern College has been a factor in the lives of many young people. I am proud to be part of his family.

There is one other person whose life has so profoundly affected me that without her, life would be an empty shell. My wife, Judy Keller Hatteberg, has quietly been the force for good in my life. If I have achieved anything, I owe it to her. Quietly, out of the limelight, our relationship grows stronger every day. She tells me who I am. She guides me down life's roads I would not take by myself.

As a teacher she influences the lives of children in more personal ways than my work, yet she shuns the spotlight. Her character is unquestioned, her goals simple: to be a good mother, wife and soul mate. She provides those of us who know her with a disciplined life that brings out the good in everyone. She has achieved her goals. Now as a writer, she is embarking down other roads that we will travel together. I cannot imagine life without her.

My daughters, Sherry and Susan, have been the highlight of my life. They are both sensitive and caring adults for whom life's promise is still golden. From this book I hope they learn it isn't money that brings happiness, or material things; instead it is relationships. People living simple lives, reacting to the world around them, and then finding ways to help others. Girls, these words are my gift to you.

This is our second "Kansas People" book. I hope the stories contained on these pages touch your life as the people on these pages have touched mine.

Larry Hatteberg
September 1994

Coming Clean

Actor Willie Aames has given up drugs and bright lights for dirt

Olathe

Willie Aames never dreamed he'd live in Kansas.

The 34-year-old actor who used to play Tommy Bradford on the popular television series, "Eight Is Enough," is a fifth-generation Californian who loves the ocean and once spent his time deep-sea fishing and racing powerboats. He also worked at Marineland Oceanarium as an underwater photographer, taking pictures of killer whales and dolphins.

Him? Move to Kansas?

"About three years ago, I would have said you were nuts. I'd have looked at you like you had three heads," Aames said.

"Kansas wasn't even a word we had ever said," said his wife, Maylo.

"Did we even know how to pronounce it when we got here?" Willie Aames added. "We spent a lot of time at the DMV going, 'K-K-K-Kan-Kan-Kan-sas.' "

But Aames knows how to pronounce the word now. And he has grown to love the state.

Aames produces and directs videos for VPR Creative Group in Overland Park, an award-winning company on the cutting edge of interactive video production. He also works as a DJ for a Kansas City-area country and western radio station. Kansas City is far from the bright lights of Hollywood, where Aames enjoyed several years of fame but came dangerously close to failure.

During his years with "Eight Is Enough," a television show about a couple raising eight children in suburban Sacramento, Aames was almost continually high on cocaine. He was a rebellious kid who gave in to the vices of Hollywood, he said, and his life, like so many other stars' lives, began to spiral out of control.

"No matter what I bought, no matter what I did, no matter what drugs I took, no matter who I slept with, and on and on and on and on and on, I could never satisfy anything inside," he said.

"And as I was sitting in a jungle in Venezuela doing a movie, doing huge amounts of cocaine, I was reading the book, 'Wired: The John Belushi Story,' " he said. "I realized what I was reading was my story. The only difference was, I hadn't died yet."

He decided to clean up his life, seeking treatment for his

drug addiction. Then he landed the job with VPR Creative group and moved with his second wife to the suburbs of Kansas City. He still uses his acting skills, doing most of the voice-overs for his company's interactive video projects.

Sometimes he misses California. But now, during occasional outings to the Pacific coast, he has a new perspective on life.

"I'm out on the boat, and you can't see anything but water, and everybody wants to know, if I love the ocean so much, why Kansas?" Aames said. "I just tell them this is the dirt version of the ocean."

He hopes his story will help others who may be dealing with drug addiction or depression.

"I was very angry, and wanted to feel as though I was part of something. And quite honestly, I wanted to be somebody's hero," he said.

His new life in the Midwest, shared with his wife and 3-year-old daughter, Harleigh, has given him that, he said.

"There is a peace about not having to keep up. I've been keeping up for almost 30 years," he said. "I'm very, very happy to live in Kansas. I love coming home to Kansas so much, and my wife loves it. . . . It is everything I have ever wanted.

"So, the more dirt, the better."

Maylo, Harleigh and Willie Aames at home in their wildflower garden.

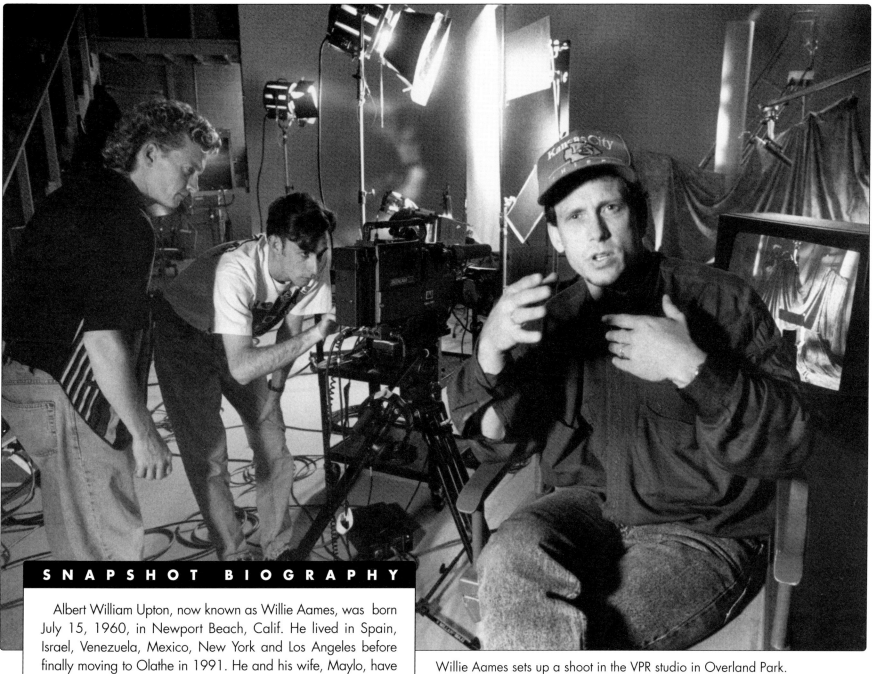

Albert William Upton, now known as Willie Aames, was born July 15, 1960, in Newport Beach, Calif. He lived in Spain, Israel, Venezuela, Mexico, New York and Los Angeles before finally moving to Olathe in 1991. He and his wife, Maylo, have a daughter, Harleigh, 4, and Aames has a 13-year-old son, Christopher, from a previous marriage. Years in Kansas: 3.

Willie Aames sets up a shoot in the VPR studio in Overland Park.

11

Bill Abell carves a wooden rose in the 130-year-old log cabin behind his home near McPherson.

Carving Out a Piece of the Past

Bill Abell returns to the old days in his restored log cabin

McPherson

Some people like modern technology, newfangled things like televisions, computers and coffeepots that start themselves.

Not Bill Abell.

For Abell, heaven is the little log cabin behind his house in rural McPherson County, where he can sit in peace in the dim light of an old kerosene lantern and think about the old days.

"If I had my choice, if my time would be up, I'd live back in the cattle days. The cattle drives and the horse days, that's when I'd live," Abell said.

"It was just open country. It was all open country and up for grabs, you know, open range. And you didn't have what we've got today — the dope and the killings — you name it, we've got it."

So Abell and his wife, Lucille, restored a 130-year-old log cabin, filling it with furnishings and knick-knacks as authentic as the cabin itself. The bed-spread, with its diamond-shaped quilt pattern, was made for a log cabin bed more than a century ago. Hanging on the walls are horse bits and bridles a friend found while plowing.

And then there's the stove.

"I had a friend at church give me that stove," Abell said. "His mother got it for a wedding present before 1900. He said he'd give it to me if I'd put it in my cabin. A neighbor went to town in 1902 and bought it and hauled it home in a wagon, and they say it weighed 700 pounds."

In this little cabin, in this wide open country, it fits right in.

"The fellow that built this cabin, he had three kids," Abell said. "He had a boy that was 14, a boy, 8, and a girl, 2. I said man, it must have been crowd-ed in here. He said when those kids got big enough to get outside in the spring, that's where they were. They stayed outside."

But Abell likes to spend time inside the cabin when he can.

"I kind of like to get away from radio and televi-sion. It's always cooler in here than going in a build-ing or shed or something. These logs out here are 10 and 12 inches thick. In the wintertime, I like to come out here and carve. . . . You know, the time passes pretty good. I could sit out here for 10 hours if I had enough coffee to drink."

He whittles for his own pleasure, to pass the time while he sits inside his cabin or outside on the porch, drinking up history.

Using nothing but a pocketknife and a slab of wood, he creates flowers, covered wagons, deer, buffalo and anything else that comes to mind.

"Oh, it's fun, but if I had to do it for a living, I'd be on the county," said Abell, who started carv-ing in 1961. "I couldn't do any good if I sold 'em. There's no money in wood carving, with all the time you spend on it. So I just save it for grandkids."

Nevertheless, his carvings have gained Abell na-tional recognition. In November 1975, representa-tives from the Smithsonian Institution and National Park Service visited Abell and took pictures of his work. Several months later, they told him he was chosen to represent the Midwest in the Festival of American Folklife in Washington, D.C.

So in the summer of 1976, Abell and his wife flew to Washington, where Abell whittled for a week on the National Mall. "It was quite a thrill for a country boy," he said. "It left us with memories we'll never forget."

And memories, for Abell, are what life is about. That's why he loves the cabin.

"It's just nice to stay out here under a kerosene lamp. The grandkids, they like to come out here, you know," he said. "My wife only stayed one time out here. That was enough for her. She said it smelled old. But yeah, I really enjoy this old thing."

History humbles him, he said. It makes him real-ize that time is short, but he'll enjoy it while he can.

"If I die tonight, I've had a good time," he said. "I asked the Lord, I said, 'Lord, if you just let me live until my kids get out of high school and get an edu-cation, then my obligation is fulfilled.' And he let me do that.

"So every day I live I thank the good Lord. I'm kinda on borrowed time, and that's the way I operate. I don't worry about things. Things don't eat on me and worry me. I just live for the day and know tomorrow will be all right. That's just the way I operate."

SNAPSHOT BIOGRAPHY

Bill Abell was born Jan. 4, 1924, in Josephine, Texas. He served in the U.S. Air Force for three and a half years during World War II and finally settled in McPherson. He and his wife, Lucille, were married in January 1948. They have three grown children. Years in Kansas: 48.

SNAPSHOT BIOGRAPHY

Darrell Albright was born Nov. 29, 1942, in Kingman. He and his wife, Joyce, were married Sept. 29, 1963, in Peabody. They have two daughters and a son. Years in Kansas: 51.

Darrell Albright is a "kid in a candy store" in the Pretty Prairie theater.

Never Say Never

Darrell Albright found home — and the Civic Theatre — at home

Pretty Prairie

It's show time again in downtown Pretty Prairie, thanks in large part to Darrell Albright.

The town's old Civic Theatre, built in 1936, closed — for good, some thought — in 1955. There it sat, quiet and popcornless, until the city, with the help of Albright, reopened it in 1981.

Years ago, nobody would have pictured Albright a man who would bring a small-town theater back to life — least of all Albright himself.

"When I left this town to seek my fame and fortune, like everybody does, there were three things I said I'd never do," Albright said. "I said I'd never come back to Pretty Prairie. I said I'd never work with the public. And I said I'd never live out in the country."

Now, along with his wife, Joyce, he has done all three. The Albrights returned to Pretty Prairie, Darrell's hometown, after living several years in Wichita, Dodge City and Topeka. They own and run the town grocery store, D&J Grocery, and live about a mile out of town, on the same rural property where Darrell grew up.

"Little did I know, everything I ever wanted was right here," he said.

One of those things is the old Civic Theatre, a musty place where townspeople used to come to watch silent films before there was anything else and classic movies before they were "classic." The last movie played in March 1955, and since then the building had been used only for occasional meetings and to show a Santa Claus movie once a year.

Albright had always wanted to run a movie house, so he asked the city if he could reopen the Civic.

He was in for a surprise.

"It needed a general cleanup. There was dirt on everything," he said. "There were some canvas side scrims that we needed, and we found those at the bottom of a big pile of stuff, all ripped and torn, so we fixed those.

"We were missing a speaker, and we found that. Then we had to find where everything plugged in, and we did, and believe it or not, everything worked pretty well."

Nowadays, for several Friday nights each spring, Albright raises the old yellow curtain, climbs into the claustrophobic projection booth and, with the help of old friends like Abbott and Costello and the Little Rascals, brings the place back to life.

"It's a lot of fun," he said. "There is something special about this place, that it has sat here so long, so empty and so quiet. To bring life back into it and to have people come and enjoy it . . . great fun."

In restoring this old place, Albright is himself rejuvenated.

"Yeah, that's exactly what it is, a kid in a candy store, except this is acceptable," he said. "Some of our vices get us in trouble, but this is OK."

The 1994 lineup was a menu of classics: "Ben Hur," "Some Like It Hot," an Andy Griffith movie called "Angel in My Pocket," a Walt Disney flick, "Gone With the Wind," and, as always, a few treats from the comedy teams of Abbott and Costello and Laurel and Hardy. Past years have featured silent movies, Westerns and even a 12-part series called "Flash Gordon Conquers the Universe."

The people of Pretty Prairie enjoy the movies, but Albright has discovered that tourists — people visiting from bigger-city places like Wichita and Hutchinson — like them even more.

"It's that same old thing, you know, people here in Pretty Prairie don't realize what they've got," he said.

Albright realizes it, though. He loves the old movies, the Civic Theatre and, most of all, this town.

"If we don't provide entertainment for ourselves, and if we don't keep our towns alive, no one from Wichita or Hutchinson or Kingman is going to do that for us. We have to do it ourselves," he said.

"The beauty of this town is that we have done that. . . . And we go home happy."

Joyce Albright serves the popcorn while Darrell runs the projector.

To Be Still

Fred Aldrich gains perspective from nature and Oriental philosophy

Perry

Fred Aldrich is trying to blend a little Buddhism with business.

At his home office in Perry, a small town just outside Lawrence, Aldrich has joined the beauty and philosophy of the Orient with life on the Kansas plains. He owns Exotica, a wholesale import business, continues to play classical piano and flute, and tries to maintain a unique perspective on life.

"I've spent a lot of time in the Orient, and I truly admire the Buddhist philosophy," he said. "What I most respect is the fact that he (Siddhartha Gautama) never sent troops into war, unlike some other leaders."

Aldrich, who majored in music at the University of Kansas, loves the simple life, watching the stars or playing his flute outdoors. You might call him a New Age man. Or you might consider his love of solitude and respect for nature a throwback to Henry David Thoreau.

In his famous book, "Walden," Thoreau wrote: "I lived alone, in the woods, a mile from any neighbor, in a house which I had built myself, on the shore of Walden Pond." Aldrich — with his self-built house, his pond and his restless mind — is re-creating the adventure of escape.

Life, for Aldrich, means "enjoying each moment of each day and all the special things that most of us let pass by," he said. "The sound of the whippoorwill and the frogs and the coyotes in the distance. And just the sound of the rippling water as it comes down the hill into the pond."

More than a decade ago, Aldrich, who owned a construction company at the time, built a Victorian-style tower on his property in Perry. It was his refuge from the world, a place where he could enjoy the quiet countryside. In 1984, a chimney fire destroyed the tower. He misses it and plans to build another one.

"I think being up in the tower, being up at that height, lends a lot of perspective," he said. "It makes all the problems of the world seem so small, when you're looking down on them.

"I think, for me, it's an expression of freedom, the freedom to be up in the air," he said. "I don't know if it's as much of an escape as it is just a place to, you know, to put things in perspective. To be still."

He put his bed in the tower, where he could watch the stars before falling asleep, and he used a crane to lift a piano up there as well. He remembers playing his flute on the balcony and watching mourning doves gather around to listen.

Aldrich's pond still exists, although a lack of rain has kept the water level low. Several years ago, he used heavy equipment from his construction company to enlarge the pond.

"I don't know if you've ever driven a backhoe, but they're wonderful things," he said. "I got going, and I just went berserk. It was fun."

Folks have been known to call Aldrich eccentric, but he doesn't mind.

"Some people seemed to interpret the tower as some sort of fortress, and that wasn't the case at all," he said. "It was just a wood building, just a way to get up and look at the world a different way. It was a place where I could play my piano and be still.

"Maybe they just didn't like Beethoven."

Fred Aldrich and Napit Atkinson at Aldrich's own version of Walden Pond.

Model for the Master

Betty Allison became one of Norman Rockwell's favorites

Wichita

The year was 1927, and a 15-year-old girl named Betty Allison had no idea she was making history.

There she sat, in a studio in New Rochelle, N.Y., her serene face the spitting image of Marlene Dietrich, while a young man named Frank Birmingham painted the words "She's My Baby" on the back of her green rain slicker. And on June 4, 1927, thanks to an illustrator named Norman Rockwell, Betty was on the cover of the Saturday Evening Post.

"When the first one came out, I was so unimpressed, I never even told the school kids about it," she said.

The first cover was titled "The Artist." After that, Allison became one of Rockwell's favorite models, appearing on eight of his Saturday Evening Post covers and one Ladies' Home Journal cover. Now living in a retirement home in west Wichita, she remembers the man who became one of America's most beloved artists.

"He was the nicest man I've ever met in my whole life," she said. "You'd never even think of him as being somebody well-known, because he was just plain ordinary people."

Allison had not even heard of Rockwell when a classmate asked if she would like to model. "He said, 'Mr. Rockwell is looking for a girl who looks kind of like you,' and I said, 'Sure, OK.' I wasn't a professional model, but he paid me fifteen dollars a day, and I felt as though I was stealing it from him."

It took Rockwell about seven days to complete an illustration, Allison says. He began by making a charcoal sketch and then would paint. Meanwhile, Betty would pose — wearing her costume and whatever expression Rockwell thought appropriate — and the artist would keep her entertained.

"All the time he was working away, and he'd be telling me stories about when he was a little boy. He had a German shepherd dog named Raleigh, and that dog would sit right beside him the whole time. He had so many stories, I'd spend most of my time laughing," she said. "He was just the most human guy I'd ever known."

Of course, she adds, he wasn't the best looking guy.

"He sure wasn't pretty to look at. He looked just like his pictures. He was tall and skiii-iny? Oooh, and had the biggest Adam's apple I have ever seen on a human being," she said. "It stuck out like a grapefruit."

But the man could paint, and some of his best known works are pictures of Allison. There's "Serenade," a picture of a young man crooning love songs to a young lady under the moonlight. And "April Showers," in which Allison, dressed in an artist's frock and holding a paintbrush in her teeth, is running to escape an afternoon rain shower. And "The Diary," which earned Rockwell a medal for best illustration of the year in 1933.

Allison keeps a book of Rockwell's collected works on the floor of her closet. It is so heavy, she can barely lift it anymore, but her eyes dance as she flips through the pages.

"This one's my favorite," she says, pointing to one called "The Yarn Spinner." In it, she is dressed in a ruffled pink gown and bonnet, and the boy

SNAPSHOT BIOGRAPHY

Betty Allison was born May 1, 1911 in Sault Ste. Marie, Mich. She moved around a lot as a child, living in Philadelphia, Niagara Falls and New Rochelle, N.Y., where she modeled for Rockwell. She married Wayne Allison in 1936, but the couple later divorced. She has two children. Years in Kansas: 2.

beside her is spinning fanciful tales of adventure on the high seas. When Allison sees it, she remembers the artist.

"We stayed in touch for a little while, and then I started working myself," she said. "I always said I was going to write to him, but I'm such a lousy letter writer, so I never did."

When Rockwell died, a piece of Allison died, too. "I just burst into tears. I really felt bad. I couldn't believe it. It was just like Peter Pan had died."

But the artist lives on in his paintings, and so, too, does Betty Allison.

"I'd do it all over, you bet," she said. "Those were some of the happiest times of my life."

"All the time he was working away, and he'd be telling me stories about when he was a little boy. . . . He had so many stories, I'd spend most of my time laughing."

"The Diary" earned Norman Rockwell a medal for best illustration of the year in 1933. It's one of Betty Allison's favorite Rockwell drawings.

The Father of the Dress

Sam Ames went from a machine shop to a bridal shop — his own

Baxter Springs

Thankful brides in at least four states have called him "the father of the dress."

Sam Ames, who once made a living grinding diesel turbos in a Baxter Springs machine shop, now makes prom and wedding dresses. It took a layoff from his job for him to begin pursuing his dream.

"When I first got started, it was really comical," Ames said, "because people would say, 'He does those?' Now it's kinda settled down."

Settled down, in part, because the dresses Ames makes are no joke. They are works of art, created with loving care out of yards and yards of taffeta, brocade, satin and lace.

"I think the thing I enjoy the most is to be able to create something that somebody else really enjoys," he said.

Pictures of smiling brides in their flowing white dresses decorate Ames' shop, and he talks about his creations like a proud father sharing stories about his children.

"I feel real proud. You kinda feel like the father of the bride in a way," he said. "In fact, I've had some of my clients that will write me notes and stuff, and they'll put, 'the father of the dress.'"

Ames began sewing in 1976, after a local woman named Juanita Gregory taught him the basics of cutting patterns, stitching and fitting clothes. "I was always interested in making things," he said, "and

I thought it would be kinda fun."

For a long time, it was just a hobby. After all, he hadn't played a part in a wedding since the 1960s, when he served as ring bearer for a relative.

Then, in 1991, he was laid off from his job at the machine shop, and he quickly went from blue collar to white lace. He still gets kidded about the unusual career change.

"They say, 'Hey, you get to fit all these beautiful women. You're around all these women all the time.' And I say, 'Well, you know, yes, but still, it's a job. You have to be very professional.

"You stop and think, of course, your big designers are men. But basically, in small towns or somewhere like that, you just don't see it."

Brides like these dresses because they're special, one-of-a-kind creations that combine the bride's personality with Ames' talent and flair.

"Each one you make, you put a little bit of yourself into it. Each dress is different, because each girl is different. Each personality is different," Ames said. "We try to bring the personality out into the dress.

"But yet, some of my personality goes into that dress, too, because there's a lot of work."

Unfortunately, some brides have to sell their dresses when the wedding is over, but Ames' wife, Rhonda, makes sure they don't sell the memory. She makes a miniature, Barbie-doll-sized replica of the dress and gives the doll to the bride as a keepsake.

"Most of the time, after the wedding, when they come back down from the wedding

and they're coming down the aisle, they'll say, 'Wow! Man, she's beautiful, Sam. It's beautiful.' That's what makes me feel good," he said.

Ames' landmark creation was a bridal gown he made last year for an Oklahoma woman. The dress, fashioned of ivory brocade with gold metallic rose patterns, had a 30-foot train. It took him about 244 hours to make and cost more than $5,000. "That was a big one," he said.

Ames also makes bridesmaid gowns and about 20 prom dresses each year. When styles change, Ames is ready, this time with sequins.

"It used to be 'Southern belle,' you know, the real full," Ames said, spreading his arms out, as if imitating Scarlett O'Hara. "But now everything is sequined and short."

This day, he is working on a red sequined dress for a local high school student. As he tacks the bottom hem with pins and fiddles with the bodice until it fits just so, the blond teenager smiles in the full-length mirror.

"Let's see, this is the third dress we've done for you?" Ames asks.

"Yes," she said, still smiling.

"OK, how does it feel?"

She nods. "Good."

And that, Ames says, is the best reward.

SNAPSHOT BIOGRAPHY

Sam Ames was born July 17, 1954, in Joplin, Mo. He and his wife, Rhonda, were married Sept. 4, 1981, in Baxter Springs. They have two children, Cassie and Joshua. Years in Kansas: 39.

Opposite: Sam Ames and Misty Kirk Burnum check with her mother during a fitting in Ames' Baxter Springs shop.

21

Mike Benewiat gives Clancy Galliart a haircut. Electronic items and ball caps cover the walls of Mike's Radio & Barber Shop in Halstead.

Keeping Busy

Mike Benewiat isn't settling for simply running a barbershop

Halstead

A barber could get bored in a place like Halstead, where life is slow and haircuts are simple.

But Mike Benewiat, the barber behind Mike's Barber Shop, found a way to pass the time and make a little extra cash on the side.

He founded Mike's Radio & Barber Shop.

You see, when there are no customers out front waiting for a trim, Benewiat repairs electronic gizmos, gadgets and anything involved with two-way radios.

"Once in a while, people make remarks about it," he said. "Never seen a barbershop have so much stuff in it."

But Benewiat can't sit and wait for the next customer to wander in. So the same hands that work the scissors and comb through Halstead's tresses rig wiring in all kinds of electronic toys.

"It makes a lazy person out of you sometimes when you get to resting too much. Not good," he said. "I feel like I like to stay busy doing something. It's interesting. Expands your mind."

Pretty unusual to have a radio repair shop and barbershop in one, you might be thinking. And you're right. But there's more.

On Benewiat's wall hangs a collection of almost 700 ball caps from all over the world. Early customers would sometimes forget their hats, Benewiat kept them, and the collection began.

"It's something I cherish because of my customers that give them to me. About 97 or 98 percent of the caps have been given to me," he said. The caps hang like windows to Kansas — a seed cap there, another one advertising a tractor, dozens more hawking products from tobacco to Chevrolets.

"I put their names in little name tags in each sack, so that someday when I retire, I can look back and say, 'Hey, I remember that customer of mine,'" Benewiat said. "That's real interesting."

His favorite cap is one that commemorated Pope John Paul II's visit to Canada, because it reminds him of his Polish heritage.

"The reason that's so important to me is that John — Pope John — and I were born within a hundred kilo-meters of each other in Poland, so it makes it real interesting for me."

So the next time you're in Halstead and have an urge to get your hair cut, have a radio repaired or gaze at an amazing ball cap collection, stop by Mike's.

"People look nice and feel better, and I just feel like I've accomplished something."

SNAPSHOT BIOGRAPHY

Mike Benewiat was born Nov. 21, 1934, in Hoczew, Poland. He moved as a youngster to Wichita to live with his father. He served in the U.S. Navy for one year. He and his wife, Mary, were married Sept. 11, 1956, in Wichita. They have four children. Years in Kansas: 45.

Mike Benewiat and his granddaughter.

She's Somebody

Juanita Blackmon believes anyone can make a difference; she does

Wichita

Juanita Blackmon, on the playgrounds of McAdams Park in northeast Wichita, is like a cross between an Army drill sergeant and Mother Theresa.

"Are you a person?" she asked one youngster, using her nail-polished fingers to pull the boy's chin toward her. "Are you special?"

"Um, well . . . " the boy stammered.

"You heard me! I said, 'Are you a person?' If you're really somebody — if you're somebody special — you'll say so."

"Well, yeah, I'm somebody," the boy said, nodding. "I am somebody!"

"Good!" Blackmon said. "Then start acting like it. Take care of yourself, and be nice to yourself. And smile!"

No sooner had the boy scampered away, joining his playmates, than Blackmon squeezed another young chin: "Are you somebody?"

You see, Blackmon believes that anyone, regardless of age, race, gender or economic situation, can make a difference in his or her community. The trick is to believe in yourself first, and then to have faith in those around you.

Blackmon was only 23 and the mother of two young children when she founded a community group called Positive Youth Making a Difference. The group, which began with Blackmon's five nieces and grew to more than 20 youngsters, picked up litter along roadsides in northeast Wichita, an area plagued by poverty, crime and violence. Its mission was Blackmon's motto: "Clean up your own house, and you are cleaning up your community. It all starts in your own back yard."

"It makes me feel good that a child feels good about himself, that he's inspired to dream or to have hope," she said.

The group thrived, and Blackmon began to earn local and even national recognition.

In 1991 she was named one of the Bush administration's "Thousand Points of Light." A framed snapshot of her with President Bush sits on a table in her house, just above an album full of letters, pictures and other mementos of her community work. She also received the Martin Luther King Jr. award from the First National Black Historical Society of Kansas and was featured on VH-1, the cable television music channel, which broadcast 60-second profiles of people who have made a difference in their communities.

Blackmon said the recognition was nice, but only because it gave her more opportunities to spread her message to area young people. She now works for the Wichita Metropolitan Family Preservation Agency, counseling young men and women about the risks of sexually transmitted diseases and teen pregnancy.

"I really feel like it created a blast of awareness about northeast Wichita, and also stirred the minds of other people who wanted to establish other programs," she said. "If they see that I can do it, then they can, too."

Although Blackmon has dedicated her life to helping others, she has faced personal hurdles of her own. Her husband of almost five years was jailed on drug charges more than a year ago and now lives with his father in Florida.

As she encourages youngsters to stay away from drugs, her home is proof of how drugs can affect families. As she counsels young women to avoid pregnancy, she is raising two children on her own. It is difficult, she said. But if she has learned one thing from her volunteer work in the community, it is that nothing is impossible.

"I feel so much relief, because I know that there is healing and sharing. And because I've been able to share my troubles, hopefully someone out there who is going through the same thing will be able to overcome the troubles that they are having."

Sometimes people ask her how she does it. How can a woman with so many responsibilities afford to spend time with people she doesn't know?

For Blackmon, the answer is simple: "Just by encouraging kids, just by giving them a job to do or helping them through school or just waving at them on the street, we're winning them. And if we win the kids, our community wins."

One time recently, a young girl asked Blackmon, "You mean you do all this work and don't get paid?"

"I do get paid," Blackmon answered. "Your smile is my pay."

Juanita Blackmon's community group helps maintain yards and encourages neighbors to take pride in their homes.

Juanita Blackmon was born Nov. 2, 1966, in Wichita. She graduated from West High School. She and her husband, Shawn, were married in 1989. She has two children — Bronson, 8, and Charity, 4. She is attending Wichita State University, working toward a degree in education or political science. Years in Kansas: 27.

Juanita Blackmon and some of the Positive Youth Making a Difference at the site of their first cleanup project on 21st Street in Wichita.

"It makes me feel good that a child feels good about himself, that he's inspired to dream or to have hope."

25

The Collector

Lee Blankinship is preserving the past in Monett's old town store

Monett

Lee Blankinship collects things.

In a remote place on a remote stretch of land where the railroad used to run, in a remote corner of Chautauqua County just outside Sedan, he preserves pieces of the past — things he hopes will keep the little town of Monett alive, at least in memory.

Some things, only history and Blankinship remember.

"This is a Sedan pop bottle. Went out of business at the turn of the century," he said, sifting through his antique treasures.

"Here's another, has a marble in it. Turn it upside down, and it won't leak. Doesn't leak one drop."

He keeps his collection in what is left of Monett's old town store. Shelves upon shelves are filled with antique hardware, toys, bottles — anything that helps Blankinship and his visitors remember what Monett was like at the turn of the century.

SNAPSHOT BIOGRAPHY

Lee Blankinship was born June 19, 1931, in Hewins. He married his wife, Carrol Ann, on April 28, 1959. The couple lives in Monett and has four grown children and 13 grandchildren. Years in Kansas: 63.

"You've got to preserve part of that stuff, or it will be gone forever," he said.

Not much of the past gets past Blankinship, whose love for the details of history prompted him to jot down his own life story. The autobiography is six typed pages of names, dates and anything else that Uel Lee Blankinship, "born the 10th child of Harvey Denton Blankinship and Mary Ethel (Schultz) Blankinship," thought important enough to preserve for posterity:

"In 1950 I bought a new Chevy pick-up for $1,400.00," one passage reads. "In October 1951 I bought a new McCullough chain saw for $380.00. It weighed at 25 lbs and had 3 hp. Wood sold then for $2.50 a rick. . . . In 1956 I got a new Chevy car for $3,000.00 and that summer I started going with the prettiest girl around. In 1957 I traded pick-ups with $1,800.00 difference."

It is the stuff of men's lives — chain saws, pretty girls and new Chevy pickups. Blankinship's collection at the old town store contains pieces of that and more. (All except for the pretty girl, that is. She likes to stay around the house.) Blankinship's "thinking place," like his memory, is an amazing destination.

"It's peaceful and content. You don't have anything to worry about here," he said.

"There are several hundred hammers here, all different types. . . . I like it where you can turn things like that, where you display it better, and it takes a lot of thinking and a lot of junk to get it that way."

Junk? Some people might think so. But Blankinship's wife, Carrol Ann — "still the prettiest girl around," he says — thinks differently. She wrote this poem:

There is a man, his name is Lee,
Who has a lot for us to see,
He likes to teach us all he can
About the life of the country man.
Every inch of space is filled,
Some of his displays are quite skilled.
Every place you look you spy
Wheels that turn and shelves stacked high.
He plans it all with such great care,
All the stories he loves to share.
It is his goal and he does strive,
To keep some of our past alive.
He restores with paint and wood,
To make things look the way they should.
The secrets of the past set free,
Done with pride by a man called Lee.

"Still have the pretty girl, the sawmill, and my home at Monett," Lee Blankinship wrote. "The years at Monett have been good to us. We have one boy, three girls, four grandsons and nine granddaughters. Over the years we have filled the store building with antiques, collectibles and the history of the area."

"I'm at home," he said. "Moved here in 1959, and when we leave here, a half-mile west is the cemetery."

Lee Blankinship is fascinated with the many old tools and appliances he collects, such as this early electric toaster.

Building a Fantasy

Beecher and Nita Brunton have another world in their back yard

Burden

"You know," Beecher Brunton said, looking around at his back yard, "when we started, we didn't realize it was going to be this big."

Without really knowing it, Beecher and Nita Brunton have built another world. In the yard behind their 100-year-old house, they planted rows of red, yellow and peach-colored roses, built waterfalls and decorated the whole thing with colorful lawn ornaments.

But they didn't stop there. Over seven years — ever since Beecher retired — they have also built a tiny church, a school and a log cabin filled with homemade dolls and other collectibles.

No special reason, they say. They just thought it would be nice.

"I call it a fantasy garden," Nita said. "I hope it's kind of a fantasy when people walk in."

Webster's Ninth New Collegiate Dictionary defines back yard as "an area that is one's special domain." Illustrating that definition should be a picture of the yard behind 619 Oak Street in Burden.

Statues of deer stand near a bubbling waterfall. Dolls with yellow-yarn hair sit on chairs or stand over washtubs in the log cabin. An American flag flutters in the wind outside the red schoolhouse. It is a peaceful, childlike place, as if someone opened a storybook and it came to life.

"I keep saying, 'Lord, why am I doing this?' " Nita said. "And I think there will be an answer someday."

Maybe the answer is in the work itself. Beecher and Nita, married for 34 years, labor together on their fantasy garden. Nita is the "architect," Beecher said, and he figures out how to make her ideas a reality.

"He helps me all the way. We're in it together," she said. "It's, you know, the companionship. And he never complains."

But Nita does her share of work in the garden, too.

"I've always liked to dig in dirt, even with my brother when he was small," she said. "With his cart, we'd dig little rows. . . . I've always been an outdoor person, although I like sewing and things. But I've always been a tomboy."

Or perhaps the answer is inside the miniature log cabin, Nita's favorite part of the yard.

"I think I like old things, and it's fun. I like to do country woodwork and stuff. But I just like the old times."

Or maybe the reason the Bruntons work so hard on their "special domain" is to see the amazement in visitors' eyes.

"If I open the gate, they're not expecting to see this," Nita said. "It's fun to watch their expressions."

Beecher speaks humbly of his efforts. No big deal, he says. All it takes is a little work every now and then. (Neither he nor his wife know how many hours they spent building this fantasy garden, and they don't feel like figuring it out.)

"People come here and say, 'Oh, it's just too much work. It's too much.' But I still maintain it isn't," Beecher said. "Why, a lot of times, we'll go nearly all week and don't do hardly anything.

"I really don't think it's all that nice," he added. "But other people come say it is, so yeah, it's all right."

Beecher and Nita Brunton have built several miniature buildings.

The Bruntons work together on their fantasy garden. She's the "architect," and he figures out how to make her ideas work.

Janitor – and Role Model

Jim Campbell has found that children make a big difference

Wichita

Children love Janitor Jim. Walk down the halls or out onto the playground at Kensler Elementary School, and it's easy to see why. Amid the chatter and chaos of another busy morning, Jim Campbell is always smiling.

"It's a lot easier to do this than be miserable," he said, greeting a line of sleepy-eyed students as they stepped off the bus and walked toward class. "It's a lot easier to be happy, and I've been doing this long enough that people expect it. So if I don't do it, I'm letting everybody down."

For 15 years, Campbell has been a janitor at Kensler. He's seen students grow up, get married and come back for a visit, sometimes bringing their own children to meet an old friend. He's cleaned a lot of lunchroom tables, hauled a lot of books and swept a lot of floors.

Not the sort of career you'd expect from a man studying for his master's degree in religious philosophy, perhaps. But then, Jim isn't your average janitor.

"The education is important for my own self-respect. I like to know I've got that ability," said Campbell, 41. "And it is another way, as a role model, that you show the kids that education is important. They see that even if your education isn't directly involved with your job, it's still important."

Campbell became a janitor because he needed the job. But since then, he has discovered that the children make a big difference.

"My wife and I can't have any kids. So this gives me 600 I can spoil every day."

Early each morning, in any weather, Campbell spends his midmorning break outside, welcoming students to school. In the winter, he reminds them to wear their hats or zip their coats. In spring and summer, he hurries them off the playground and into the building in time for the first bell. If they're getting off the bus, he reminds them to be careful, and if they get a ride to school, he reminds them to kiss Mom or Dad before rushing to class.

"I like to feel I'm a part of the educational process. I think we all are. It's just one of those things listed on your job description as 'et cetera,' " he said, chuckling.

For the students at Kensler, Campbell is as much

a part of school as math problems and morning announcements. Inside his office, which is little more than a large broom closet, he keeps kazoos, yo-yos and other trinkets to brighten grouchy faces, and his door is decorated with a crayon portrait that says, "Janitor Jim. He keeps our school clean. He is our friend."

"They got the ponytail right," Campbell said, pointing to the drawing and tugging his long strands of hair. "Even if it's just a stick figure, they remember the ponytail."

First-grade teachers have recruited Campbell to help teach the concept of zero to their students. On every 10th day of school, he dresses up in a purple mask and cape and plays "Zero Hero," visiting classrooms to help students count by tens.

"A lot of the children don't have a particular male role model, and in elementary schools there aren't that many men teachers. They need to know that men can be teachers, and men can be happy being janitors, and I have a lot of pride in that," he said.

"And it reflects in the kids. They see you're happy with your work. They see you're proud in your work. And I like to be that example for them, too."

Campbell also dedicates free time to the kids. He took a vacation day recently to accompany students on a field trip to the Cosmosphere in Hutchinson.

"What people usually remember me for isn't on my job description," he said. "But when you see them play and you know they're happy, well, inside I know I've done my job right."

Jim Campbell has been a janitor at Kensler Elementary School for 15 years.

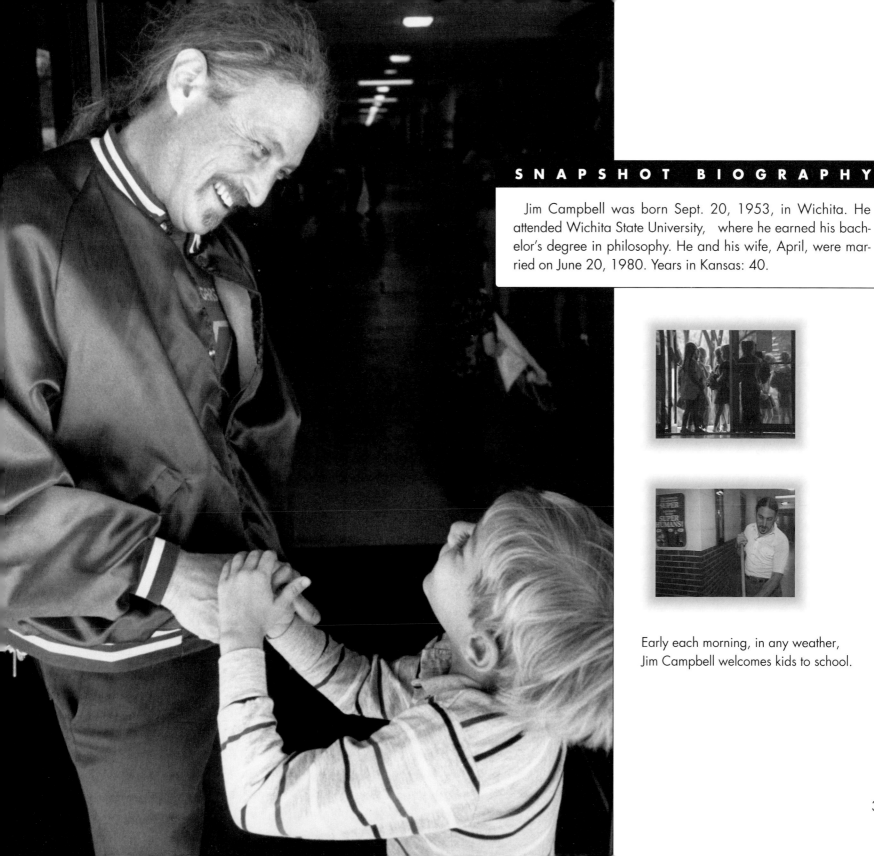

SNAPSHOT BIOGRAPHY

Jim Campbell was born Sept. 20, 1953, in Wichita. He attended Wichita State University, where he earned his bachelor's degree in philosophy. He and his wife, April, were married on June 20, 1980. Years in Kansas: 40.

Early each morning, in any weather, Jim Campbell welcomes kids to school.

Puncturing Politicians

Richard Crowson uses humor like a scalpel in his editorial cartoons

Wichita

When Richard Crowson was 4 years old, sitting in a pew of the Evangelical Methodist Church in Memphis, Tenn., he thanked the Lord for sharpened pencils.

"That preacher would give Bible-thumping, hell-fire-and-brimstone sermons, and the whole time, I'd be drawing," Crowson said. "I think it was kind of a defense mechanism.

"I'd sit there quietly and draw crucifixion scenes. I know that sounds terrible, probably, but that's what I did."

Now he uses his God-given talent and devilish wit to capture less divine subjects. Namely, politicians.

As editorial cartoonist for The Wichita Eagle, the state's largest daily newspaper, Crowson uses humor to titillate, to embarrass, to expose and to make readers think.

"A good cartoon is one that gets people's pulse pounding and also gets them engaged in an issue," he said.

"There's something real primal about that graphic

Richard and Karen Crowson sing and play blue-grass music around the state.

image. Everything's right there in black and white. Right or wrong. Good or bad. There's no gray area. It's as simple as you can get, and it's something words on paper can't do."

Crowson began his career drawing scathing caricatures of his high school algebra teacher. He went on to contribute editorial cartoons to the student newspaper at Memphis State University, where he earned his bachelor's degree in history, and then for The Jackson Sun in Jackson, Tenn. Today, his renditions of presidents, governors, Kansas officials and city leaders have attracted state and national attention.

What does he love most about his job? Tweaking the noses of those in power. Especially big, round, easy-to-draw noses.

"Every now and then, when you get a caricature just right, you get this kind of rush," he said.

"You know how the Indians say they don't like to be photographed, because they believe the picture robs them of a little bit of their soul? Well, it sounds weird, but I believe a good editorial cartoon does that, too. For just a minute, you feel like you've got this power over that person, like you've really captured them on paper."

Creating good editorial cartoons takes more than a steady hand and sharp wit, Crowson said. It also takes an understanding of complicated political issues and the ability to whittle them down to their core, to a basic idea that readers can grasp in an instant.

During the 1990 race for Kansas governor, Democratic candidate Joan Finney was continually criticized for dancing around — or, rather, smiling around — serious issues. A Crowson cartoon showed a scene from "Alice in Wonderland," with

Alice asking, "What's your position, Mrs. Finney?" and Finney perched on a tree limb, grinning like the Cheshire cat.

"I truly felt like the reason Joan Finney was elected was for me," Crowson said. The governor's toothy grin makes her an editorial cartoonist's dream. "I did something really good in a former life, and now I'm being rewarded."

There are others he likes to draw, too. President Clinton, for example. And Ross Perot. Kansas Rep. Dan Glickman. Even former Vice President Dan Quayle.

But don't ask him which, out of the hundreds of cartoons he has drawn, are his favorites. "That's kind of like asking a parent which kids he likes best," he said.

"I like them for different reasons. Some I like because they hacked off a lot of people. Others I might like because a lot of people liked it."

In 1988, a Crowson cartoon — one depicting former Sedgwick County Commissioner Dave Bayouth and former County Manager Kim Dewey clad in diapers, sitting in high chairs, slinging "baby feud" — prompted a public apology from Bayouth.

"It was like getting cold water thrown in your face," Bayouth said during a news conference, holding up a copy of the cartoon.

Crowson said rewards are seldom so visible. More often, he fields angry phone calls from cartoon subjects, "when venom is just dripping from the phone, forming puddles at my feet." Even then, he tries to keep things in perspective.

"I try to say, 'Look, it's only an editorial cartoon. It's just lines on paper,'" Crowson said. "And most of the time, people are pretty good sports."

Richard Crowson, editorial cartoonist for The Wichita Eagle, does some of his work at home, where he can also help care for Haley.

Wayne Dunafon, who began ranching for himself in 1940, rests after helping bring a calf into the world.

Marlboro Man

When Wayne Dunafon quit making cigarette commercials, he quit smoking

Westmoreland

"**Y**ou've had your supper and coffee. The horses are settled down. You settle back. You start to think about Saturday night in town. You watch the sun slide down the sky 'til it's just a big red ball. And if you sit real still and listen, you can almost hear the evening fall."

If you remember that Marlboro television commercial, with a handsome young cowboy smoking his cigarette and watching the sunset, then you remember Wayne Dunafon.

Dunafon was the Marlboro Man — a roping, riding, cigarette-smoking piece of Americana. Thing is, he wasn't acting.

"My life as a rodeo cowboy and a rancher and so forth had molded me more or less into what the Marlboro Man is," Dunafon said. "I don't have to act or anything, I just do what I normally do as far as horses and cattle and ranch business is concerned."

Wayne was 5 years old when his parents moved in a covered wagon from Nebraska to Russell. After high school, he worked for several years on ranches in Colorado before moving to Westmoreland to begin ranching for himself in 1940.

His only possessions were $7 and a saddle. (Lori Dunafon, Wayne's wife of 36 years, always thought "Seven Dollars and a Saddle" would make a good title for a story about her husband's life.) For transportation, Dunafon took care of young horses and broke them to ride for local farmers and ranchers. For cash, he would go into Westmoreland on Saturday nights and win $10 for getting on any horse that "couldn't be rode."

Like many young ranchers, Dunafon began competing on the rodeo circuit and traveling the country. In 1956, he was runner-up to the world champion steer wrestler. But it was during a monthlong rodeo in New York City that Dunafon began modeling on the side. His handsome face and macho physique landed him jobs advertising Lee Rider jeans, Firestone tires and Chevrolet pickups.

"It was a way to make some extra money, that's the way I saw it," Dunafon said. "But everybody back home was happy for me and real proud."

Marlboro representatives discovered him during a rodeo in Cheyenne, Wyo., in 1964. The company wanted real cowboys, they said, for an ad campaign that would pair Marlboro with the macho image of the Old West. Dunafon became one of a series of actors and models who wore cowboy garb to pitch Marlboro cigarettes.

Marlboro officials may not have known it at the time, but Dunafon had been the Marlboro Man several years earlier, modeling for a different kind of campaign.

"They had me once in a little sports car," he said, "and one time wearing a smoking jacket."

A what?

"Yup, I wore a velvet smoking jacket. That wasn't me at all."

But in the later commercials, Dunafon was at home. He wore his own shearling coat, chaps and Stetson hat, and clutched a cigarette ever-so-casually in the left corner of his mouth. Atop a chestnut quarter horse — usually one he borrowed from a local cowboy — he helped move cattle on some of the biggest ranches and amid the most beautiful scenery in the West.

After cigarette commercials were banned from the airwaves in 1970, Dunafon went back to work full time on his ranch in Westmoreland. He also quit smoking. It was part of a deal he had made with his son, Douglas.

"When Doug was in the fifth grade, someone came to his school to talk about how bad cigarettes are for you, and he came home all concerned," Dunafon said. "And I told him then, 'If I don't make these commercials, somebody else will. But as soon as I stop making these commercials, I'll stop smoking.' So that's what I did."

But Dunafon never stopped ranching, and he is still a card-carrying lifetime member of the Professional Rodeo Cowboys Association. These days, he rides pickups more often than horses, and works within gates and fences rather than on the wide-open countryside. He likes it just the same.

"I'm not an actor. I don't have to be," he said. "I just do what's natural."

Wayne Dunafon and his grandchildren.

SNAPSHOT BIOGRAPHY

Wayne Dunafon was born June 15, 1919, in Yuma, Colo. He attended high school in Russell and worked several years in Colorado before moving to Westmoreland, where he began ranching for himself in 1940. He and his wife, Lorraine, have two children and four grandchildren. Years in Kansas: 65.

SNAPSHOT BIOGRAPHY

Dale Dunn was born Oct. 17, 1929, in Burlingame. In 1957, he earned his bachelor's degree in education from Kansas State Teachers College, and in 1967 he earned his master's degree in education administration from Wichita State University. He and his wife, Karen, have been married 28 years and have two children. Years in Kansas: 64.

Dale Dunn enjoys being out in the sunshine, mowing and trimming lawns.

On the Cutting Edge

Dale Dunn traded a career in education for a lawn mowing business

Wichita

As principal at Wilbur Junior High in Wichita, Dale Dunn used to run a school of 800 students and a staff of 75.

Now he pushes a lawn mower. He likes this new phase of his life.

"There's not much stress to this job," he said. "And teaching, for me, was not stressful until the last two or three years. It seemed to change then, but then maybe I'm the one who changed.

"I used to wake up in the middle of the night and plan what I was going to do for the next day and stay awake. I don't do that anymore. In fact, I sleep late now, so I'll stay out of the way of the wife and daughter."

When the school system offered Dunn an early retirement in 1990, he left education and joined the lawn mowing business his son Kip was running at the time. There are those who tell him he's wasting his talents, but he just takes that as a compliment.

"I think some people thought I wouldn't do this, but I've always enjoyed physical labor," Dunn said. "It's a nice change for me, and, of course, the nice thing about it is, I don't have to do it if I don't want to."

But he wants to. Dunn enjoys being out in the sunshine, grooming and trimming lawns like an artist who wants to make each new creation a masterpiece.

"My wife says now she doesn't understand how I could have held down a full-time job, because I'm so busy now, I don't have time to do all the things I have planned," Dunn said, smiling.

But education was his life, and he admits he misses it sometimes. As he mowed a lawn in south Wichita, he recalled how he used to wipe down the lunchroom tables at Wilbur because it kept him in touch with the children. His boss didn't like it.

"I wiped the tables until the new superintendent came, and he thought that wasn't what a principal ought to be doing," he said. "But I knew it worked for me, so I kept doing it.

"I cleaned up after a lot of kids, but it paid off for me."

His new brand of manual labor pays off, too. But this, he said, is a good bit quicker.

"I like this. When you get through, you get some immediate satisfaction," he said. "When you're cleaning up after kids, sometimes it takes a long time to see the results."

And because Dunn mows lawns the old-fashioned way — "I'd rather get the exercise than sit on that (riding) lawn mower" — he's discovered another result. While many retirees relax at home, Dunn has gotten back into shape and is already down to his Marine Corps weight of the mid-1950s.

In 1994 he served as interim principal at Sedgwick Elementary School. He had fun, but mowing lawns is his life now, and he's happy.

"Yes sir, I sure think I am anyway."

Dale Dunn served as interim principal at Sedgwick Elementary School in 1994.

Visionary

Wayne Elliott is finding adventure in running a sawmill

Elk Falls

It's raining in Elk Falls, a small southeastern Kansas town of about 130.

And inside Wayne Elliott's sawmill, it's raining cedar shavings.

"I tease my wife, I call it a vision, and I'm a visionary," said Elliott, a middle-aged man who owns and runs an old-fashioned sawmill. "Other people are dreamers and different things. I'm a visionary.

"Of course, the whole sawmill and everything here was a vision at one time. But we're working toward it, and it's turning dreams and ideas into realities."

The rain, the remote location, the slow pace of life — all are reasons that Elliott decided to put a sawmill in Elk Falls. He moved to Elk Falls in 1975 after hearing about the town through a co-worker at a construction site in Tulsa.

"I came to spend a weekend here, just to relax and visit, and I fell in love with the place," he said. "Now it's home."

Elliott built the sawmill in 1990. At the mill he processes and dries wood that is native to southeast Kansas, selling some and using the rest in an adjoining woodworking shop, where he builds cabinets and furniture.

"There's plenty of work to do," he said. "But it's nice to shut the equipment off and listen to the rain on the tin building. I've always enjoyed that."

As a circular saw buzzes, sending wood shavings flying like snowflakes in a blizzard, Elliott smiles. He was born to be in Elk Falls.

"I look at this as like pioneers. I relate back to the pioneers. They were adventuresome," he said. "This is my adventure. It's exciting at times and scary at times. Will this succeed?

"Yeah, it's adventuresome. But sure, it's going to

succeed. People have to have a positive attitude if they're going to reach out for adventure."

There's nothing new in this sawmill but the wood. All the equipment was used generations ago, when sawmills were the building blocks of pioneer towns. Back then, you couldn't drive down to the big lumberyard to pick up a few two-by-fours; instead, you came to a place like this.

"There's a lot of people that are trying to capture the 1890s again," Elliott said.

Part of Elliott's dream is the feel of the wood against his fingertips, the smell of the cedar shavings.

"Wood is an amazing material, in the sense that it has different strength qualities," he said. "Every log has its own grain. Sometimes I just stop and I look at the wood, because it's totally unique."

This sawmill is unique, too. Behind the mill, Elliott has built a small gift shop, where his mother-in-law, who lives nearby, occasionally hosts demonstrations of old-time soap-making.

He's also building a large barn, and sometimes local fiddle, banjo and guitar players perform bluegrass music on a makeshift stage.

At Elliott's sawmill, there is a use for everything, just like the old days. Out of hedgewood comes hedgewood sawdust, a fine yellow powder that Elliott calls "Kansas Gold."

"They extract it, and it makes a beautiful yellow die," he said, pouring the sawdust

into a bucket. He ships most of the hedgewood dust to California and Washington.

Hang around Elliott's sawmill long enough, and you understand the appeal of the simple life — simple business, simple town, simple people. "It's enjoyable living here," he said.

"In January, me and my friends grabbed the fishing poles one day and went out, and my friend caught a seven-and-a-half-pound bass," Elliott said, then emphasized the point, as if he couldn't believe it himself. "In January!"

The sawmill is Elliott's passion and his way of life. And like the strong wood he transforms into planks, boards and "Kansas Gold," he is turning something ordinary into something glorious.

"This is going to succeed, somehow, some way," he said. "I believe in it."

Wayne Elliott's sawmill turns hedgewood sawdust into "Kansas Gold."

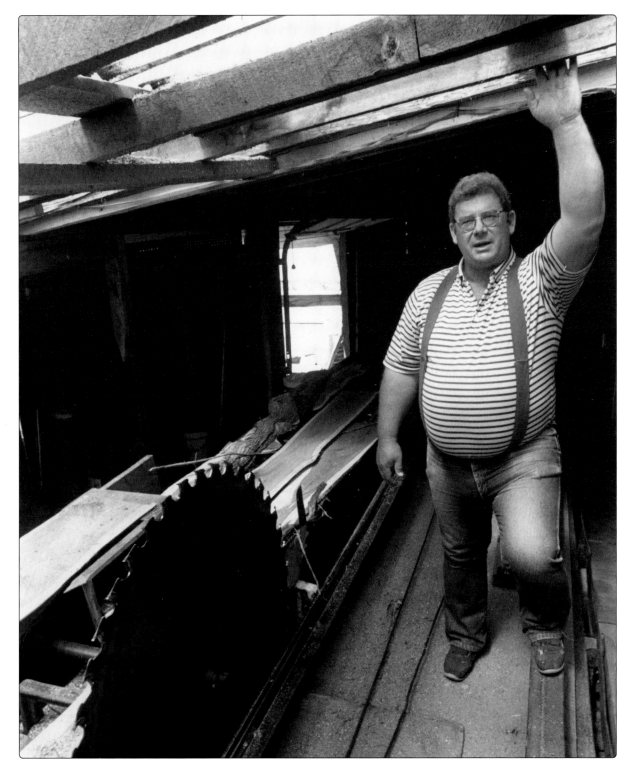

SNAPSHOT BIOGRAPHY

Wayne Elliott was born Jan. 28, 1949, in Hutchinson. He grew up in the Hutchinson area and graduated from Nickerson High School. After high school, he worked various construction jobs throughout Kansas and Oklahoma. He moved to Elk Falls in 1975 and worked construction until 1990, when he built the Elk Falls Sawmill. He and his wife, Charlene, were married Jan. 26, 1980, in Elk Falls. They have one son. Years in Kansas: 41.

Wayne Elliott believes his sawmill is going to succeed.

"Of course, the whole sawmill and everything here was a vision at one time. But we're working toward it, and it's turning dreams and ideas into realities."

Lighting Up Christmas
Dean Gamble's Candy Cane Lane warms visitors' hearts during holidays

Greensburg

For most of the year, Dean Gamble's place on the north edge of Greensburg looks like your typical western Kansas farm.

It has a barn, a silo, a windmill and acres of land planted to wheat in the fall, milo in the spring.

But for 10 evenings each December, just after the sun sets, Gamble's farm turns into a winter wonderland called Candy Cane Lane. More than two dozen Christmas displays — all of them covered with lights and most with moving parts — have caught the eyes and lifted the spirits of thousands of visitors.

Gamble started his Christmas display in Stafford in the early 1960s, when he taught math and sci-

ence at the local high school and lived across the street from the town hospital. His display was modest back then — a few strands of lights and some lighted Santa Claus figures — but the neighbors loved it.

"The patients at the hospital got such a kick out of watching it go up," he said. "The holiday season is a heck of a time to spend in the hospital, so it felt good to make them smile."

He returned to his hometown of Greensburg in 1973, at the height of the energy crisis, when Christmas displays were discouraged. "It was a couple years before I started up again," he said. "But it's been up every year since then, and it continues to grow."

Combining his knack for rigging motors, gears

and pulleys with his love of the holidays, Gamble creates mechanical lighted displays that bring Christmas to life. He begins setting up the display on Thanksgiving Day and flips the switch for the public two Saturdays before Christmas.

"My wife used to get calls from retirement homes asking what day we were going to turn on the lights," Gamble said. "They can't wait for the show."

And what a show it is. Along Gamble's U-shaped driveway is a snowman that tips his hat, two elves in a snowbank, and Santa Claus waiting to take off in an airplane, waving to visitors as the plane's propellers turn. Another display flashes "Peace on Earth" in big, bright letters, and another shows Santa blasting off in a rocket.

On the south side of the drive is a display titled "What a Wreck," which Gamble designed and built several years ago.

"Santa has had a mishap in his sled, see," Gamble explained. Beside the wrecked sleigh, a flustered reindeer tries to reattach one of its broken antlers while Santa thumbs for a ride.

Candy Cane Lane gets its name from a quarter-mile stretch of 4-foot-tall lighted candy canes that greets visitors from an old pasture just south of Gamble's house. But the hallmark of the display is a 50-foot-tall red candle with a flickering orange flame, constructed of lights and standing in front of the silo. On a clear December night, you can see it for miles.

All around the driveway, decorated street signs direct

cruisers to Sleighbell Avenue, Toy Shop Street and other imaginary destinations. And for several evenings each year, a real-live Santa Claus welcomes visitors, and Mrs. Claus gives each person a candy cane as he drives away.

Gamble said all his time, work and increased electric bills are worth it when he sees the smile on a visitor's face.

"You get more enjoyment from getting on one of those rest home buses and handing out candy canes when you see their faces light up and smile," he said. "Maybe their kids are 1,000 miles away, or maybe they're in town but never come to see them.

"From the look on their faces, it's just like you've handed them a thousand dollars. That's why I do all this."

He does it because he loves Christmas, and he knows the magic and wonder it can bring.

"I try to make Christmas happier for everybody, because as you well know, there is a lot of sadness in the world at Christmastime," he said. "It makes my heart glad that I can wish people in our community a merry Christmas."

Hundreds of animated figures fill Dean Gamble's yard during the Christmas season. "I try to make Christmas happier for everybody," he says.

Mary Gourlay was born Nov. 15, 1932, in Wellington. She attended Wichita State University for three years before marrying her husband, Robert, in August 1953. They have five children. Years in Kansas: 55.

Mary Gourlay gets plenty of exercise at the Bartlett Arboretum during tulip season.

Another Green Thumb

At Bartlett Arboretum, Mary Gourlay continues her parents' work

Belle Plaine

How could anyone drive by the Bartlett Arboretum on a clear spring day and not peek inside for a look at those tulips and pansies?

Mary Gourlay can't figure it out.

"It gets discouraging when everything starts to look so beautiful and no one comes to see it. All that work, and, 'Aw, shoot,' " Gourlay said.

Aw, shoot, indeed. If anybody needed a good reason to get off the Kansas Turnpike, this is it. Since 1910, when Gourlay's grandfather turned 15 acres of marshland into an island of trees, shrubs and beautiful flowering plants, the Bartlett Arboretum has been one of the state's best-kept secrets.

Gourlay's parents inherited these quiet acres, and the arboretum became Mary's life.

"We used to have a lily pond down here at the other end of the fountain," Gourlay said. "And when my folks weren't around, my girlfriends and I would go swimming in there with the goldfish."

When her folks were around, discussions almost always turned to gardening.

"Truthfully, I got tired of listening to the conversations about trees at every meal," she said. "But something must have rubbed off, I guess."

After her parents died, Mary took over the arboretum, and her husband, Robert, quit his sales job to help. How difficult a task is it? Just ask Mary. (She's the one on her hands and knees in the dirt.)

"People pay good money to get exercise like this," she said. "We plant 30,000 tulips and about 5,000 pansies. When you plant 5,000 pansies,

there's an awful lot of old pansy blooms to be picked off every day, let me tell you. You've got to have good thumbnails."

And in the fall, 15 acres of trees shed an awful lot of leaves.

"My husband and I rake the whole thing," she said. "A lot of people ask, 'How big a crew do you have?' and they can't believe it's just two people

Robert and Mary Gourlay greet guests at Bartlett Arboretum.

doing it. . . . Lots of times I'd like to get in the car and just go on a vacation, but we don't think about that until winter."

Sometimes it is hard work just reading the weather report and praying that the bad stuff dodges Belle Plaine. Lucky for the Gourlays, the Euphrates Creek runs through the arboretum, supplying enough water for several species of trees that are unique to Kansas. But the creek dries up during unusually hot, dry summers, and sometimes it floods its banks and destroys the gardens. Other times, vicious thunderstorms or early-spring freezes are the enemy.

"Every time we hear there is hail in the vicinity, I just get cold chills. . . . Or sometimes, 'Oh, no, it's going to freeze, and it will hurt this and it will hurt that.' But that's nature, and you can't do anything about it."

But like a third-generation keeper of a family farm, Gourlay takes pride in continuing the work her parents and grandparents started.

"You've got to spend all your waking hours doing it. It's very labor intensive. . . . We just keep persevering."

And when this island of color begins to bloom, when the gardens explode in color and butterflies fill the air, Gourlay knows it's all worth it. She just wants other people to enjoy it as much as she does.

"I think everybody is too busy. They've got too many things to do, too many places to go. They don't take time to enjoy nature," she said. "But that's what life is all about."

Wild Man

Bob Gress is devoted to teaching others about nature

Wichita

"**I**s that a hoot owl?"

The lady with silver hair and curious eyes drilled Bob Gress almost immediately, as soon as the first slide of his presentation beamed onto a portable screen in the auditorium of the Prairie Homestead retirement home. The picture showed the logo of Wichita Wild, a park department nature education program that Gress oversees.

"That's a great horned owl," Gress explained, still fiddling with the slide projector. "There's really no such bird as a hoot owl."

"You mean, they don't go, 'Hoot, hoot?'"

"Well, they all go 'Hoot, hoot,'" Gress said, smiling. "You're absolutely right."

With a loaded slide projector, a sense of humor and "special friends" such as Digger the badger, Webster the beaver and Squirt the skunk, Wichita's wildlife naturalist brings nature into the classroom. And whether the students are grade-school youngsters or retirees, the message is the same.

"The more we learn and the more we know about this amazing system called Earth, the more we care for it and protect it."

After earning bachelor's and master's degrees in biology from Emporia State University, Gress began his career studying peanuts for the Agricultural Research Service in Oklahoma. It wasn't long before he realized his real place was out among the red-tailed hawks and white-tailed deer, observing wildlife and teaching others about nature.

Not that he had anything against peanuts.

"I had a wildlife biology background, and I wanted to work with wildlife," he said. "This job opened up with the city, and I said, 'Yeah, that's what I want to do.'"

He is now the director of Wichita Wild, a conservation and education group that oversees nature areas at several city parks, as well as the Kansas Wildlife Exhibit in Central Riverside Park. Gress spends much of his time doing educational programs, teaching people about the natural habitat they often overlook — their back yards.

"Oftentimes, we Kansans know more about animals in Africa, South America and Australia than we do about the ones right here," he said.

"We hope that with these programs, they learn that, 'Hey, Kansas does have some important things to teach us about nature.'"

His presentation at the Prairie Homestead retirement home illustrated the delicate natural balance between predators and prey. People often scorn snakes and spiders or feel sorry for animals that are killed for food, Gress said, but they don't realize how well nature works.

Did you know, for instance, that a certain species of field mouse in Kansas reproduces so quickly, two mice could parent enough generations to produce more than 1 million offspring in only a year? Without bats, snakes, raccoons, possums, owls and other predator animals, we'd be overrun with rodents, Gress said.

The audience listened intently, groaning when Gress described earthworms as "mole spaghetti" and cringing when he said caterpillars were not only a nutritious meal for box turtles, but nice and juicy, too. "People like animals until they have to eat," he said. "That's not very fair."

Like most presentations, this one ended with one of Wichita Wild's "special friends" — a golden eagle named Aquila. Several years ago, the eagle was shot by a hunter in Wyoming, and he never recovered enough to fly; like Gress, he now serves to teach people that nature must be protected. Watching the noble bird perched on Gress' elk-skin-gloved arm, it is easy to see why the naturalist loves his job.

"Our hope is that more of us learn that the golden eagle is a part of our natural world and certainly deserves to live there," he said. "We need to take care of what we have."

SNAPSHOT BIOGRAPHY

Bob Gress was born Jan. 22, 1952, in Axtell. He graduated in 1970 from Axtell High School. In 1974 he earned his bachelor of arts degree in biology from Emporia State University and two years later received his master's degree in environmental biology. He and his wife, Mary, were married Oct. 8, 1977, in Paola. Years in Kansas: 42.

Bob Gress at Chisholm Creek Park in Wichita. He is director of Wichita Wild.

Buster's Place a Different World

That's the way Buster Hathaway likes it

Sun City

The Coors beer logo and a sign that says, "OPEN. Pepsi-Cola" are all that distinguish Buster Hathaway's bar from the rest of the chipped-paint, dusty buildings of downtown Sun City. Outside his window, a summer wind sweeps over the Gypsum Hills of Barber County.

But come inside, and it's a different world.

"It's a different world, all right," he said. "But that's the way I like it."

This is Buster Hathaway's place. For 50 years, Buster's been the man behind the counter here, where ranchers, folks from the nearby gypsum mine, men from the oil fields and the occasional tourist stop by for burgers and beer.

"What else can I get you boys?" Buster asks. It is a frequent refrain.

"I want a hamburger."

"Hamburger." No pencil or notepad here, only a nod. "One, two, how many?"

"One. I'm on a diet."

"That's three cheeseburgers. Do I hear four?"

If you've met Buster once, you'll be back. You'll come for the beer, served in frosty glass mugs you can hardly lift, or to see the stuffed bobcat that monitors the dining room. You'll come to hear the story of Buster's mother-in-law, a sharp-eyed American Indian who condemned alcohol in public, then asked Buster to pick her up an extra bottle of liquor next time the bootleggers came around. You'll come for stories, food and company.

You'll come to experience Buster's Place — that's what he calls it, for lack of a fancier name — like coming home to a place you've never lived.

"Well, after 48 years in here, don't you imagine, probably, it's just kinda like home?" he said. "And I do have to do something to stay busy. If I didn't, I'd be nuttier'n a fruitcake."

Bring your wife. Bring your children. They'll be treated with respect.

"I don't tolerate a lot of vulgarity and cussing and screaming and hollering," Buster said. "Shut the door easy when you leave. That's always been my theory."

Shut the door easy, and don't be too fussy about toilets. Because if you've gotta go at Buster's Place, you've gotta go out back.

"This is a WPA public toilet," he said, walking toward the frazzled wooden outhouse behind his bar. Inside is a toilet, all right. But don't expect modern frills like a soft, cushiony toilet seat, or a flusher, or heat.

"Well, we have had women who said they couldn't use it. . . . I said, 'Wait long enough, and you can.' People are nuts."

Buster's is a man's place, you see. A place where some things are just understood. An "ideal beer," for instance, is poured from a keg into a frosty glass mug, and the frothy head — who said less is better? — is scraped off the top with a table knife.

"There's an ideal beer," Buster said, holding up a sample. "If there isn't any head on it, you don't get no taste."

And as much as you might admire Buster's mugs,

Two bobcats monitor Buster Hathaway's place.

please, don't ask to take one home.

"One woman came in here and offered my wife two hundred dollars for one of 'em," he said. "She looked at her, and she said, 'Lady, I don't need your money. I need the glass. Thanks anyway.'"

Coming to Buster's place in Sun City is like shaking hands with an old friend. Of course, Buster's almost as good at being humble as he is at pouring beer.

"I hope you understand my sentiments. There's nothing important about me. Why worry about it?" he said with a grin. "I'm no legend, after all. I'm just Buster."

And with that, he added, "Hurry back."

SNAPSHOT BIOGRAPHY

Buster Hathaway was born March 1, 1919, in Yuma, Colo. He moved to Sun City in 1943, shortly after marrying his wife, Alma. Alma Hathaway died in 1991. Years in Kansas: 51.

Huge beer glasses and a "This is not Burger King" sign are among the accoutrements of Buster's place.

47

The Grannie Behind the Mustard

Lydia Hein has turned a family recipe into big business

Hillsboro

The ingredients are listed right on the bear-shaped plastic bottle: ground mustard seed, vinegar, salt, spice, turmeric, sugar, flour, water and dry mustard.

But the recipe for Grannie's Homemade Mustard is top secret, so don't even bother asking.

"It's a recipe that was handed down to me from my sister," says Lydia Hein, a retired dietary aide who, at age 63, began producing and selling jars of the famous-recipe mustard out of the basement of her double-wide mobile home. "I had been making it for 20 years before I started doing this."

Now Hein, the "Grannie" in Grannie's Homemade Mustard, is stirring up big business along with the sugar, flour and turmeric.

"Never in our wildest dreams did we imagine that we would be in 90, almost 100 grocery stores in Kansas, 50 gift shops, gourmet shops, some in Oklahoma, Pittsburgh, Massachusetts, Jackson Hole, Wyo., and Colorado," she says.

And never in her wildest dreams did she think she would start a business at an age when most folks are thinking about retiring.

"Nobody in his right mind would do that," she said with a coy smile. "But I had to quit my job because of my health, and I asked the Lord, 'What do you want me to do now?' and he said, 'Go with your mustard.' So I have followed him."

It began in September 1990, when her youngest son, Eugene, persuaded her to make a batch of the tangy-sweet mustard to sell at the Hillsboro Arts & Crafts Fair. "He kept begging and begging, 'Why don't you make some of that mustard and sell it?' and I said, 'I'm not going to make a fool of myself.' "

But she made a batch anyway, filled a few jelly jars and sold $100 worth of mustard the first day.

The following year, customers from as far away as Texas returned to the Hillsboro fair to buy mustard, and Hein's business took off. Before long, she and her husband, Emice, built a state-approved kitchen in their basement, rigged a four-gallon mixer to a makeshift bottling contraption, and Grannie's Homemade Mustard was in full production.

Originally, the whole family — Lydia, Emice, and their four grandchildren, Kendall, Kimberly, Kendra and Keevan — worked together to prepare, package and label the mustard. But as business grew, the Heins hired two retired women, Ruby Friesen and Betty Duerksen, to help with production. Now the mustard

Emice Hein, Ruby Friesen and Betty Duerksen help Lydia Hein complete an order of Grannie's Homemade Mustard.

is sold in shops from New Jersey to California.

When she first started the business, Hein said, she remembered Matthew 13:31-32: "The kingdom of heaven is like to a grain of mustard seed. . . . Which indeed is the least of all seeds: but when it is grown, it is the greatest among herbs." The Heins like to think of their business that way — a gift from God that has grown beyond their dreams.

"I just thought at the time, 'How in the world would anybody want to buy mustard?' " Emice Hein said, laughing.

"Are you laughing now?" asked Lydia.

"No, I am not."

These days, the sharp smell of jalapeno powder fills the Heins' basement, where boxes of quart-size glass jars and 8-ounce plastic squeeze bottles wait to be distributed. The jars — some filled with original "sweet and tangy" mustard and some with the recently developed "hot" recipe — carry the "Land of Kansas" label and a UPC code, which allows the small-time mustard to be sold at big-time grocery stores.

Some big names have tasted Grannie's mustard. Sen. Nancy Kassebaum served Grannie's at a senators' luncheon in Washington, D.C., and Russian President Boris Yeltsin took some home after his visit to Kansas in 1992. Hein sent 16 cases of the mustard to Bloomingdales for use in a Kansas food promotion, and she filled at least one order for the Pentagon.

What makes Grannie's mustard so special?

"I think people like it because it has a tang to it," said Hein. "It isn't so flat. It's really different."

So, too, is Grannie. And customers like it that way.

SNAPSHOT BIOGRAPHY

Lydia Hein was born Aug. 31, 1928, in Buhler. She and her husband, Emice, were married in Buhler on Sept. 29, 1947, and later moved to Hillsboro. They have three sons, four grandchildren and three great-grandchildren. Years in Kansas: 66.

Lydia Hein's mustard kitchen is in the basement of her rural Hillsboro home.

Bank Job

Patrycia Herndon wants to bring back an old building's grandeur

Dighton

In 1981, Patrycia Herndon visited the Lane County Historical Museum to see what she could learn about an old bank building in downtown Dighton. Herndon, an artist, had bought the building at 421 E. Long because she needed more space to create and display her paintings, and because she appreciated the old building's timeless, if a bit rickety, beauty.

It was the beginning of an obsession.

"All of a sudden, in my mind, I could see it as it was back in the 1800s," Herndon said. "All those stories and those scenes just started coming to life."

That is how Herndon became a weekend historian and preservationist. Her goal is to restore the old bank to its original grandeur, to discover its secrets and share them with others.

Like the story about the bandits from Oklahoma. (Schoolchildren love this one, Herndon said.)

In 1922, three men from Oklahoma began working at the bank. They told townspeople that they were repairmen who specialized in fixing office machinery. But their real goal, as residents discovered later, was to get inside the bank, learn how it operated and where the money was stored, and steal all the money.

"What they didn't know was that there was an alarm system hooked up to the vault," Herndon said. When the thieves tried to break into the vault with a crowbar, the alarm sounded and an old-time adventure began.

Residents chased the robbers through the dusty streets of Dighton and into the vast countryside, and after several hours, the thieves seemed to disappear. No one could find them.

Enter a 10-year-old girl named Wiletta Finkenbinder. According to newspaper reports,

Wiletta, who had been playing cops and robbers with a group of friends, had climbed to the top of a windmill tower. From there, she spotted the three bandits hiding in a field. Townspeople surrounded the men and, after a brief shoot-out, killed one thief and captured his two cohorts.

Old copies of The Dighton Herald and The Lane County Journal show photographs of the dead bandit's body lying on the sidewalk in front of the bank, a gruesome example of what attempted robbery could get you in 1922.

Little wonder, with stories like that, how Herndon could become a voluntary prisoner of history. She spends weekends at the museum, looking through microfilm in search of anything that mentions the old bank. Meanwhile, with the help of townspeople who remember the bank and some who have even saved artifacts from the building, she is restoring it to its turn-of-the-century glory.

"Some of them, I'm sure they think I'm crazy," Herndon said. "But I think most of them are glad I'm doing this."

One time, an elderly woman stopped Herndon in the grocery store check-out line and asked if she was the person "rebuilding that bank." Turns out, the woman had an old burglar alarm in her basement — the one that was installed in the Dighton bank in 1906 and later helped catch those three Oklahoma bandits.

"Those are some of my fondest discoveries, the nicest and most special to me," Herndon said. "It's an ongoing adventure."

On the bank's second floor, the adventure continues. A corner room that Herndon now uses for her studio was once a dentist's office.

"And before I had finished cleaning the room, I

had found this many teeth," she said, holding up a small jar full of turn-of-the-century molars, canines and incisors. "It looked like the dentist used to pull teeth and then just toss them over in the corner."

Recently, Herndon enrolled in a woodworking class at Garden City Community College in hopes of learning how to repair and, in some cases, rebuild parts of the bank. She is now building the teller's cage, using the original top, columns and trim. For her, a Texas native, the research and restoration work have made her feel right at home in western Kansas.

"I feel like I've been here ever since this community was organized in 1886, because I feel like I know these people, even though I never met them," she said. "It makes me feel like I belong. I feel kinda like I've got roots way down deep."

Patrycia Herndon uses a room at her bank gallery as a studio.

SNAPSHOT BIOGRAPHY

Patrycia Ann Herndon was born June 1, 1939, in Bailey, Texas. She earned her bachelor of science degree in costume design, fashion illustration and art education from Texas Woman's University in 1961. While in college, she met and married Walter Herndon, and the couple later moved to Dighton. They have two children. Years in Kansas: 33.

Restoring the bank gallery is an ongoing adventure for Patrycia Herndon.

Model Maker

Jake Hiebert has fashioned a collection of miniature machines

Whitewater

People do different things when they retire. Some do unusual things. Some do crazy things. Some don't do anything at all.

Jake Hiebert, retired farmer, carpenter and self-described jack-of-all-trades, decided he'd build himself a collection of miniature farm machinery.

"This is what I growed up with, so I started this after I retired," Hiebert said. "A lot of people go bowling and stuff, but this is my hobby, and this is what I did."

With carving tools and pieces of wood or tin, Hiebert fashions miniature versions of farm implements and other machines from the 1920s, '30s and '40s. His collection includes tractors, wheat cutters, wagons, a windmill, a Model T truck, a grain storage bin and a four-horse stagecoach.

His wife, Mary, paints the models, putting the farmers in traditional blue overalls and coloring the horses brown, black or dapple-gray.

The Hieberts take the display to area festivals, wherever organizers will give them the space to set it up and the time to share their stories with passers-by. During the past several years, they have traveled to schools and senior citizen centers throughout Kansas, and their display won a Best of Show plaque two years in a row from the National Association of Belt Buckle Collectors.

Many of the visits take place on Kansas Day, when teachers want to show their students what old-time Kansas farmers used to work with.

"We've showed them at nursing homes," Jake Hiebert said. "When you show them at a nursing home, you don't have to start a conversation. Their memories go right back. And if they don't have a memory, they'll get one."

The models fill an upstairs bedroom in the Hieberts' house in Whitewater. The largest model is an old-fashioned combine with belts that move when you plug it in.

"It was a 14-foot cut, so the combine is 14 inches wide," Hiebert said. "I put chains where there was chains, and rubber bands where there was rubber belts. It's a challenge, but I enjoy it."

Hiebert was legally blind when he started his hobby in 1983. His failing eyesight forced him to quit working as a carpenter, but he could still carve pieces of wood in his hands. In 1984 he received a cornea transplant and now sees much better.

Still, a team of unusually thin workhorses sits in one corner of the bedroom, the product of early experiments.

"My horses were too skinny," he said. "They needed some oats."

"He makes them bigger now," Mary added. "They look better."

Hiebert spares no time or expense in making his models historically accurate, right down to the genuine leather harnesses on the horses. Sometimes he works from pictures or drawings, sometimes straight from memory. Building a 1933 model combine, for instance, was a cinch.

"I cut a lot of acres with that one," he said. "I knew where every bolt and screw went."

Hiebert said he can't think of a better way to whittle away time after retiring. So he'll keep on carving scrap wood into pieces of the past.

"I've got my little work area out there in the garage, and I don't bother anybody. I like it."

Jake Hiebert carves horses and Mary Hiebert paints them on the porch of their home in Whitewater.

SNAPSHOT BIOGRAPHY

Jake Hiebert was born Dec. 9, 1912, in Lehigh. He and his wife, Mary, were married April 14, 1937, in Newton. Hiebert spent most of his life farming, but made a living during the Great Depression by doing carpentry work, digging wells and being a jack-of-all-trades. Jake and Mary have two children and four grandchildren. Years in Kansas: 81.

Jake Hiebert makes miniature farm machinery, such as this combine.

Still in the Saddle

Pete Hiebert is helping keep the Old West alive and riding

Pete Hiebert's job is getting cowboys back in the saddle again.

"It's an old-time job. But then, so is riding horses," Hiebert said. "I kinda like that, though. I enjoy it."

In his garage-turned-workshop just outside Peabody, the smell of leather hangs in the air. Hiebert makes saddles and bridles by hand — the old-fashioned way — and his work is known and respected by cowboys, ranchers and horse enthusiasts nationwide.

SNAPSHOT BIOGRAPHY

Pete Hiebert was born March 21, 1913, in Hillsboro. A farmer and rancher, he worked three years at Sheplers Western Store in Wichita, repairing saddles and other tack. He now lives outside Peabody, where he runs his own tack business. Years in Kansas: 81.

He starts with a metal frame, the "saddle tree." Around and over the frame, he stretches sheets of quality cowhide leather — about "two sides" of leather, or an entire cowhide, for every full-sized saddle. His hands are slow and sure as he hammers the leather and trims it clean. After decades at this job, he knows what works.

"It's got to set right on the horse," he said, running a hand over the frame. "And then the top has to be formed right so the guys are comfortable, because the guys spend their whole day in the saddle."

At one time, Hiebert spent his days in the saddle. He was a farmer and rancher, raising wheat along with his prize quarter horses. Watch him work, and you're taken back to a time when everyone depended on his horse and saddle — for work and play.

"Nature has always been fascinating to me. I like the outside," he said. "I like animals. Animals have life, and life is what it's all about."

Most of Hiebert's saddles are simple, not the ornate, rhinestone-studded kind you see in rodeos and Hollywood movies. The seat is plain and smooth, with only a bit of decoration, and the sides are stamped with his signature, "P.H." These are the saddles of real cowboys.

"If you're riding all day on a ranch or a feedlot, you don't want a lot of stuff on there to rub. That's what causes saddle sores," he said. "They like 'em real plain. It's practical."

The stirrups are similarly basic, a metal bond covered with rawhide. "They last almost indefinitely," he said.

Not to say that Hiebert doesn't create his share of leather masterpieces. Just recently, a recreational horseman from Madison, N.J., ordered a saddle from Hiebert, and the artist embellished it with fancy stitching and stamps.

One of Hiebert's saddles will cost between $1,000 and $1,200. But as his customers know, the money is well-spent — and usually spent only once.

"When we make them, they are completely handmade, no machine work done on 'em. . . . They don't come undone when we're through with it."

Hiebert also repairs saddles; it's the majority of his business, in fact. Day after day, he replaces aged, cracked seats with soft leather, making them feel and smell like new. He likes this part of his job, he said, because he feels like he is preserving the past.

Part of his workshop is dedicated to antique saddles, ones he has collected from friends and customers through the years. Among them is a side-saddle built in 1806, a cavalry saddle complete with saddlebags, an old pony saddle and one used by a German soldier in World War II.

Also in the collection is a saddle with so much fancy stitching and adornments, you can hardly see the leather. "That one almost talks to you, doesn't it?" Hiebert said, smiling.

That one isn't quite his style, he admitted. But to each cowboy, his own.

"Those there are for the drugstore cowboys," he said, lifting a pair of shiny silver spurs. "You know, the ones who just come in and rest their boots on the drugstore rail."

Whether plain or fancy, Hiebert is content knowing that his saddles keep the Old West alive — and riding. "These are for people who want something they can depend on," he said. "And it's sort of remembering the past. I like the past."

The saddles that Pete Hiebert makes sell
so fast that he can't keep one in stock.

55

William Howe's butterfly paintings have been exhibited at the Natural History Museum in Dyche Hall at the University of Kansas and at many other places.

Chasing Butterflies

William Howe has been entranced by them since he was 11 years old

Ottawa

William Howe has spent his life chasing butterflies. It is a wondrous, beautiful existence.

"I've been more or less enslaved to them for a long, long time," he said.

It began when Howe was 11. His father, a cotton entomologist for the U.S. Department of Agriculture and Plant Quarantine, brought home a batch of caterpillars one day, and young William watched, entranced, as the insects formed their mummy-like chrysalides. Later, when the quiet cocoons transformed into black and yellow swallowtail butterflies, he was spellbound — and hooked.

"I thought, 'My Lord, that's a magnificent looking thing,' and from then on, I was just hooked on butterflies," he said. "Didn't matter what it was. I guess you just say I just fell in love with them, literally."

Howe's fascination for butterflies, combined with an artistic talent and creative flair, have resulted in some of the most beautiful, detailed paintings of butterflies ever created. His paintings, in watercolor and acrylic, permanently capture a sight most people see only in the flash of time it takes a butterfly to land on a flower, spread its wings and flutter away.

Now he is known as "the Butterfly Man," and his illustrations have been published in such books as "Our Butterflies and Moths," "North American Wildlife" and "Mariposas de Mexico." Another book, Doubleday's "The Butterflies of North America," included illustrations of about 2,000 species of butterflies, and took Howe seven years to complete.

The work, he says, is a labor of love, from running through fields with his net to meticulously re-creating nature's art on his canvas.

"I caught this one out in the Chippewa Hills last spring," he said, holding up a zebra swallowtail, its wings outspread to reveal perfect black and white markings. The Chippewa Hills, near Howe's home in Franklin County, are a prime spot to see butterflies, he said. "I don't make up any butterflies. They are all done from actual models."

Because of this, the work takes intense concentration. He wants every stripe, every spot, every splash of color to be as vivid as nature intended.

"You're almost like on another planet," he said. "If the phone rings, it just shatters you completely. You're just detached from reality. You do get almost lost in it."

His studio is nothing fancy, just a cluttered room in his Ottawa house, which was built in the 1850s. But these creatures — striking Southern dogfaces, zebra swallowtails and Daunus swallowtails, with wings that blossom into perfect, symmetrical colors — may be some of the fanciest on Earth.

One of Howe's paintings, titled "High Surreal Noon," is an adaptation of a Daunus swallowtail he found during one of his regular butterfly hunting trips to Mexico. An arch of butterfly wings, with the entire swallowtail displayed in the center, depicts the cycle of the sun — from cool, green morning to bright yellow noonday and coppery red sunset. "Just like an enchanting evening at San Miguel Regla," he said.

In addition to illustrating wildlife books and manuals, Howe's work has been exhibited at the Smithsonian Institution, the Museum of Anthropology, the Los Angeles County Museum, galleries in New York's SoHo district, the Carnegie Museum and many universities in Kansas and elsewhere. He was named Kansas Artist of the Year in 1987.

In 1988, Howe donated his collection of more than 10,000 butterflies to the Los Angeles County Museum. He said he didn't have time to maintain the collection, which can be infested with bugs, and he was through studying the scientific aspects of butterflies. Now, with about 2,000 butterflies to use as models for his paintings, he focuses on the art.

"There's really no end to it. There hasn't been so far," he said, adding another dash of color to his painting of the zebra swallowtail. "There's nothing else I'd rather do."

SNAPSHOT BIOGRAPHY

William Howe was born June 18, 1928, in Stockton, Calif. He moved to Kansas when his father, an entomologist, took a teaching position at the University of Kansas in Lawrence. He attended the Kansas City Art Institute and School of Design and received his bachelor of arts degree from Ottawa University in 1951. Years in Kansas: 52.

The Farmer's Wife

Alberta Hubele always had a taste for the country life

Gypsum

When Alberta Hubele was a little girl, all she wanted was to be a Roy Knapp Rough Rider.

Like those lucky children who performed trick riding stunts on Knapp's team of Shetland ponies, Alberta wanted to stand on the back of her own pony, one hand holding tight to the reins and the other waving to the audience. She wanted to feed her pony and bring it sugar cubes for snacks.

But Alberta Hubele grew up in a small house in Kansas City, Kan., with a small yard that didn't have

Joy and Thad Hubele grew up enjoying grandmother Alberta Hubele's farm.

enough room for a dog, much less a pony.

Every now and then, she would visit her aunt and uncle's farm near Lawrence. She and her cousins would build boats and ride them on the Wakarusa River, which flowed through the farm. Then they would sit on big flat rocks along the river's edge and run their hands along names, initials and Indian designs that were carved there.

"I remember that so clearly, and I was just an itty-bitty girl," Hubele said. "Ever since the first time I went out to the farm, I determined I was going to marry me a farmer."

She found one when she was just out of junior high school. During a visit to her sister and brother-in-law's farm, she met the boy who lived down the road. He was good-looking, she remembers. But that wasn't all.

"I remember, one of the first things that impressed me was one time, he was up in a hayloft, and there was a big ol' snake," Hubele said. "He just grabbed that thing by the tail and cracked it like a whip, and the head snapped off and went flying.

"I thought, 'Oh, my goodness, what is this?' It didn't impress me as being romantic or anything like that, but it sure was interesting."

In 1938, she married that boy, Eugene Hubele, and moved with him to a farm in Gypsum. Together they raised wheat, milo, Hereford cattle, chickens, hogs and just about anything else that Alberta wanted.

Once, she adopted a particularly sweet-tempered hog, named him Wilbur and kept him as a pet. He grew to be 700 pounds — so big that when he lay down, he couldn't get up on his own. Eugene had to fire up the tractor, scoop him up with the front-loader and set him on his feet.

"I guess it was kind of peculiar," Hubele said. "It got to where neighbors wouldn't really say hi to me. They'd just say, 'How's your hog?'"

Hubele also raised several orphan calves, sometimes keeping them on the porch so she could bottle-feed them easily. On cold winter nights, she brought them inside and laid them in the bathtub.

"Eugene never complained. In fact, he liked the help," Hubele said. "I can't think of anything else I'd rather do."

Of course, rural life wasn't always easy or fun. Eugene Hubele lost a leg in a farming accident 25 years ago, and two of the Hubele's four children died, one shortly after her birth and another in 1990. In November 1993, Eugene died, too.

"Anyplace you live, you're going to have rough times. I lived in the city during the Depression, and we had rough times of making it," she said. "But I love it here. There are so many advantages, and to me, it's the only place to raise children."

These days, Hubele's chickens follow her around the yard, picking at her feet, and her two dogs, Dolly and Ginger, keep her company inside the house. One of her sons, Adrian, still farms the Hubeles' land, and his two children grew up in the country, living the life Alberta Hubele always dreamed about. They even had Shetland ponies to ride.

A few snakes still crawl into the basement every winter, and because Eugene never taught her how to kill them, Alberta lets them stay. "My trick is just to keep out of the basement," she said.

Yep, she loves the country life — triumphs, tragedies, snakes and all.

"I sure intend to stay here," Hubele said. "I'd rather live 'til I die right here."

SNAPSHOT BIOGRAPHY

Alberta Hubele was born Oct. 3, 1921, in Kansas City, Kan. She and her husband, Eugene, were married for 55 years before he died in November 1993. The couple had four children, one of whom died shortly after birth and another who died in an accident in 1990. Alberta has five grandchildren and one great-grandchild. Years in Kansas: 72.

Alberta Hubele has a variety of animals on her Gypsum farm.

Survivor

Shawn Huff wants to help children who suffer the way he suffered

Sterling

There are times Shawn Huff can still feel the abuse — the electrical cords, baseball bats and angry hands hitting his young body. There are times he hears the cruel insults: "You're no good. . . . You're ugly. . . . You'll never amount to anything." Sometimes he can even smell the anesthetic.

It took 22 operations to repair the physical abuse Huff endured from his biological parents and two foster families. Abuse and neglect claimed his right eye when he was only 3 and then stole most of the hearing from his left ear.

But thanks to adoptive parents who rescued him from his nightmare, to teachers who believed in him, and to his unending faith in God, Huff has survived.

"I had nothing to smile about. I cried every day," Huff said. "My world was very dark, very gray, very rainy, and I couldn't find a way out.

"But somehow, through all of that, I always thought, 'Maybe. Maybe things will get better. Maybe something good will come along. Maybe. Maybe.' "

He was 6 years old when Stephen and Sharon Huff, a childless couple from Minot, N.D., flipped through books full of snapshots and saw Shawn's picture. Officials told them about Shawn's tragic past, and they warned them that the child's emotional scars were even deeper than his physical ones. He had "behavioral problems," they said. He had trouble getting along with adults and other children.

That, Shawn says, was an understatement.

"I swore. I threw desks at teachers. I tried to stab teachers. I was so angry inside," he said. "I did things that would make most parents say, 'That's it. You're gone.' But they never gave up on me.

"Every day, I praise God for whatever it was that made my parents pick me out of that thick book of kids."

After moving to Colorado Springs, Colo., with his new family, Huff attended Hilltop Baptist High School, where he excelled in sports. His football coach helped him discover Christianity. Other coaches and teachers convinced him that those years of abuse and neglect were not his fault.

"I spent many hours in a time-out room with a teacher holding me and saying, 'Shawn, I love you.' And I'm crying and kicking and saying, 'I hate you,' " Huff said. "I think those times were building bridges. Those were building-block times, knocking down the walls of my life."

By the time he moved to Kansas to attend Sterling College, he knew he wanted to help other children who suffer the same kind of abuse and neglect. He is majoring in family studies and hopes to become a counselor.

Meanwhile, he travels the state, talking to church groups, schools and other organizations about his past and what it takes to overcome adversity. In 1992, he was honored as one of President Bush's Points of Light, and he traveled to Washington, D.C., to meet the president.

"Whenever I speak, I don't try to paint this picture of the perfect person. That's not what it's about," he said. "I just try to give hope and to challenge people to think about where they stand now with that higher power.

"Because no matter what you might say right now, things are always changing. Like the sun rises in the morning, things change, and there'll be new challenges to face. You have to be strong enough to have faith during those times when things are bad," he said.

And because he is black, Huff says, his message is twofold.

"I've spoken in a lot of small towns, where the only perception they've ever had of minorities is what they see in the news, and that's not always good," he said. "If I can visit with them and share how I overcame the adversity in my life, it changes their perception about minorities in general."

Huff is a survivor, and he hopes others can learn from his experiences.

"There's an old saying my coach told me: If you aim at nothing, you're bound to hit it. And I always remember that," he said. "Have a goal. Don't set your goals to win awards. Set your goals on firm foundations, and keep the Lord first, and those other things will come."

Shawn Huff shares stories with Sterling teammate Bernie Silvers Jr.

SNAPSHOT BIOGRAPHY

Shawn Huff was born Jan. 20, 1972, in Corpus Christi, Texas. After being abused by his parents and two foster families, he was adopted by Stephen and Sharon Huff, of Minot, N.D. The family soon moved to Colorado Springs, Colo., where Shawn graduated from Hilltop Baptist School. He moved to Kansas in 1991, after receiving a football scholarship to attend Sterling College. He is a senior majoring in family studies. Years in Kansas: 3.

Shawn Huff is majoring in family studies and hopes to become a counselor.

61

Frank Jensen has created 28 metal sculptures, which he displays just east of Augusta.

Henry's Sculpture Hill

The artworks are his, but his name isn't Henry — it's Frank Jensen

Wichita

Atop a hill in central Butler County, a giant praying mantis is ready to pounce on an unsuspecting grasshopper.

Pan, the mythical Greek god of pastures, flocks and shepherds, is playing his flute, leading a parade of happy children.

Grendel, the monster from "Beowulf," is devouring a victim, Macbeth's witches are gathered around their caldron, and mighty Casey has struck out.

This is "Henry's Sculpture Hill," a collection of 28 metal sculptures created and displayed by artist Frank Jensen.

Most of Jensen's works follow literary themes. Some are fashioned out of old farm machinery parts. All of them show Jensen's subtle wit and unmistakable style.

"This is probably where I belong," said Jensen, a retired high school English teacher. "I own the hill, and if someone wants to come by and look at it, fine. If not, that's fine, too."

The hill is an open field dotted with clusters of trees and metal sculptures. It is adjacent to U.S. 54, just east of Augusta. Although Jensen lives with his wife, Julia, in Wichita, he regularly spends mornings and weekends on the hill, where he has a roomy workshop, a barn for storing old sculptures and works-in-progress, and a refrigerator stocked with Coca-Cola.

The artist doesn't talk much about himself or his work, opting instead to hand visitors a sculpture-by-sculpture guide to the hill and let them judge for themselves.

"I figure people might want to talk with each other about the sculptures, and I don't want to stand around in their way," he said. "I say go out on your own, and if you have any questions, I'll be here."

But although Jensen may not accompany you on your walking tour, his subtle, folksy sense of humor is evident nonetheless. This is his written description of one work, "The Three Graces," which depicts women dancing:

"Aglaia (brilliance), Euphrosyne (joy), and Thalia (bloom). Because their original names are difficult to pronounce, I call them Ethel, Helen, and Babe. Babe is in front."

Other descriptions include excerpts from well-known writings by John Milton, William Shakespeare, Geoffrey Chaucer, William Carlos Williams and John Keats.

Jensen's style is as diverse as his subject matter. Though all his works are made of metal, some forms look open and airy, like skeletons, while others have angular, flat surfaces.

"One good thing about not being famous," he said, "is that I can do whatever I want."

One of the most instantly recognizable sculptures in the collection — and the one most motorists spy from nearby U.S. 54 — is "Don Quixote." The scene depicts the Man of La Mancha astride his horse, Rocinante, bravely but foolishly charging a windmill that he believes to be a monster. His companion, Sancho Panza, lags behind, trying to dissuade Quixote.

"There are many men from La Mancha with the impossible dream," Jensen wrote in his guide.

Some might say Jensen's artistic career is an impossible dream, and even Jensen downplays any recognition he receives. For instance, the "Henry" in Henry's Sculpture Hill is a mysterious character who Jensen says is the one who really creates the sculptures.

"If I told you that the guy responsible for all this was someone who looked like me, would you believe me?" he said, smiling. "I've got to explain it somehow."

Perhaps visitors to the hill — and even Jensen himself — should heed the 19th-century English poem, "Ode on a Grecian Urn," by Keats:

"Beauty is truth, truth beauty — that is all / Ye know on earth, and all ye need to know."

Jensen with Don Quixote charging a windmill.

Rebecca Copley Johnson practices opera roles before an animal audience at the Johnsons' Smolan farm.

The Voice

Rebecca Copley Johnson's talent has taken her around the world

Smolan

These Smoky Valley hills are alive with music, and the only audience is a herd of Hereford cattle.

"Swing low, sweet chariot," Rebecca Copley Johnson begins, her crisp soprano voice filling the fields. "Comin' for to carry me home. . . . "

It is a voice that has awed opera audiences around the world and inspired critics to sing her praises:

"There is only one word to describe the performance given by soprano Rebecca Copley," a New Jersey newspaper reviewer once wrote. "The word is splendor. This is a voice that can rise like the sun right through chorus and orchestra, dead on pitch, and hang there gleaming."

This particular afternoon, in Johnson's little hometown on the Great Plains of central Kansas, it is gleaming for the cattle. They continue chomping their hay.

"One time, I was going to make my debut at the New York City Opera in the role of Turandot, by Puccini," she said. "And we had a whole herd out there on the grass, and it was so beautiful, and I just started."

Again, she demonstrates the voice that has made her one of the most gifted young opera vocalists in the world. Notes rise and float and linger like seeds blown from a dandelion. Cows and steers raise their heads and turn toward her.

"And all the cows stopped, just like they're doing over there."

It's not what you'd expect to hear in the rolling hills of Smolan, excerpts of operas by Mozart, Puccini, Verdi and Wagner. But this is where

Rebecca Copley Johnson got her start. Her father is the late Elmer Copley, who once directed the well-known and respected music department at Bethany College. Rebecca attended Bethany herself, earning her bachelor's degree with honors in music.

"This whole area has taken an interest. The Smoky Valley, this area, is very important to me," she said. "It keeps me centered. It keeps me grounded."

She is on the road much of the year, singing in such opera capitals as Paris, New York and Vienna. Her husband, Don, meanwhile, stays home in Smolan and minds the cattle. Sometimes they meet in a faraway place so he can watch her perform.

"When I see the reaction she gets from the crowds, it makes it all worthwhile," he said.

"Buildings are great. Cities are great. I love traveling and meeting people," Rebecca said. "But I need to be outside in God's world."

In operas, she has played the roles of Tosca, Aida, Desdemona and Mistress Ford, among others. At home, she is just herself. And that, she said, is something to sing about.

"I'm so lucky, and yet that's not the be-all, end-all," she said. "Being here together with Don, the rest of our extended family, that's what's important. Taking care of what we have.

"I'm living a fairy tale. I really am."

SNAPSHOT BIOGRAPHY

Rebecca Copley Johnson was born Jan. 29, 1952, in Moline, Ill. Her family moved to Lindsborg in 1960, and she attended grade school and high school there. She earned her bachelor of arts in music from Bethany College. She married her husband, Don, on Nov. 28, 1987. Years in Kansas: 34.

Harry Kaufman was born Aug. 1, 1890, in Pratt County. He completed the seventh grade in a four-room schoolhouse in Hartford. When he was 12, he moved to Milford, Neb., where he met and later married his first wife, Annie Boeckner. They were married for 59 years and had five children. He married his second wife, Erna Schmidt, on May 11, 1979, in Newton. They were married two and a half years before Erna died. Years in Kansas: 96.

Harry Kaufman turned 104 in August 1994. He still loves to sing, play the harmonica and tell jokes.

A Century of Learning

Harry Kaufman is 104, but he's not worried about getting old

Hesston

On Aug. 1, 1994, Harry Kaufman turned 104.

He's still not worried about getting old.

"There's a paper that comes here about aging, and I don't get nothin' out of it, hardly," he said. "It just goes in the wastebasket."

A couple of years ago, Kaufman sat down to write about his life. The eight-page document, written in a bold, cursive scrawl, begins, "My life story — I will start out with my Dad. His folks were old Amish in Holmes County. . . . "

It continues with facts, stories and the lessons of life.

At a school in Beaver Crossing, Neb., for instance, Kaufman learned what happens to chatter-mouth little boys.

"I was so bad to whisper, they had me sit in the teacher's chair. That didn't work, so the teacher had me stand in a corner, face the rest. That didn't work, so she had me hold out my hand and hit it with a ruler.

"That didn't feel very good, but it done the work."

Kaufman's long life is its own lesson. He says the secret to long life might be his diet.

"Well, it's fruits and vegetables and nuts and seeds — sunflower seeds, they're great. Alfalfa, that's great. The alfalfa plants go way down and bring up vitamins and minerals."

No meat. No bread. But don't let anyone tell you that no work is good for the life span, Kaufman said.

"Some say you don't want to work too hard. Well, I'm never afraid of that," he said. "I think that's what helps you digest your food."

Kaufman lives at a retirement home in Hesston known as The Villa. Only a few years ago, though, he was still living in his house a few blocks away.

He took care of his own garden and walked to The Villa every day, just to visit.

"I always say a brisk walk is good, good exercise," he said.

Today, he visits full time and plays his harmonica. He learned to play the soulful instrument when he was just a kid, waiting for church service to start.

"We had thirteen miles to church, but Dad never liked to be late. He was generally the first one after the janitor," he said. "The church was against music in the church, so a number of us boys had harps. The first song I learned to play was 'Nelly Bly.' "

Over the past several years, Kaufman has performed for school groups and other organizations in Hesston, Goessel, Walton, Moundridge, Hutchinson and Newton. "I play and sing a lot at The Villa, 'til they get the old folks in for the programs," he said.

As a child, Kaufman said that when he grew up, he would play his harmonica in a band. So far, that hasn't happened.

But there's still time.

Harry Kaufman even plays the harmonica while riding an exercise bike, something he often does three times in a day.

Jack Kellogg's Wichita Hat Works has one of the best collections of hats anywhere.

Hatman Jack

Jack Kellogg is a topper when it comes to hats

Wichita

The woman who walked into Jack Kellogg's hat shop had a saucy voice and a penchant for wide brims.

"I like this one. I'll try it on," she said, and she did. Then, looking in the mirror, she said, "Can you snap this brim over my right eye just a little bit?"

"Well, I certainly could," Kellogg answered.

"You know why I'd like to do that, don't you?" she said.

"No, I don't."

"Well, when I'm dancing with my husband and my hat's snapped over my right eye, he can't see that I'm looking at other men."

"You know, I thought I'd heard all the stories," Kellogg said. "But that tops 'em all."

Anyone who knows anything about hats — fedoras, top hats, bonnets or bowlers — knows "Hatman Jack." And they know that he tops 'em all.

Kellogg grew up in Wichita, and he grew up wearing hats. Big western hats with high crowns and wide brims, Tom Mix style. After graduating from high school and studying business and marketing at Wichita State University, he knew what he wanted to do.

"I just loved hats, and everything I did kept coming back to hats," he said. "Before long, I learned to make hats, and the business was a natural transition."

Today, Kellogg's small shop, Wichita Hat Works, has one of the best collections of hats anywhere, and his workmanship is recognized nationwide.

Tri-Star Pictures recently ordered 15 custom-made hats for "The Quick and the Dead," an old-time Western starring Sharon Stone. Costume designer Sarah Edwards wanted one of the hats to look 100 years old — "like it had been rode hard and put away wet," Kellogg said — so he tarnished it with oil, dirt, rusty nails and just about anything

else he could find. The Hollywood folks loved it.

Few people leave Kellogg's store disappointed. That's because he insists that there's a hat for everyone, and if you give him a chance, he'll find one for you.

"Everybody has a shape that looks good on them," he said. "Every hat you try on will serve to show you in a different way, or even accentuate something different about you.

"I figure, no matter what it is you wear, if it's flashy, if it fits you, if it looks good, buy it."

Some of Kellogg's hats are practical, some are outrageous. Some are worn to imitate the stars — Fred Astaire, Charlie Chaplin, Garth Brooks, Jackie Kennedy. And some, like one fashioned from a rubber inner tube and old flannel shirts, are just too wacky for Kellogg to pass up.

"There's a guy in Wichita who makes these," he said, "and I just had to have one in my store."

Much of Kellogg's business is taking worn-out hats and, with a little cleaning or a new ribbon, making them look new again.

Of course, some people don't want them to look new again. A man came into the store recently, holding his weathered fedora like a crown, and told Kellogg it needed a little "fixin' up." The beige felt hat was covered with brown stains and splotches, its ribbon was frayed, and the sweatband was all but completely torn apart.

"I don't want you to clean it or anything," he told Kellogg. "I just got it to where I like it."

"Well," Kellogg said, turning the old hat around in his hands. "We'll see what we can do."

Hatman Jack helps Bob Heasty pick out a hat.

SNAPSHOT BIOGRAPHY

Jack Kellogg was born July 28, 1958, in Wichita. He graduated from North High School and attended Wichita State University. He opened his first hat shop in Wichita in 1977. He and his wife, Cheryl, were married Oct. 16, 1993. Years in Kansas: 36.

For Kellogg, seeing a worn-out, well-loved hat is like reading its owner's life history. Repairing it is an honor. And always, with the next customer who comes in the door, there's another story to tell.

"One time a guy came in from western Kansas, and the underside of his hat brim was completely burned. The leather was shriveled," Kellogg said.

Turns out, the cowboy had branded a calf too soon after spraying him with flammable medicine, the cow had caught fire, and the nearest thing the cowboy could find to extinguish the flames was his hat. After a special "Hatman Jack" repair job, though, the hat was like new.

And the cow?

"Medium rare."

Always Listening

As town dispatcher in Conway Springs, Marvin Kibbe is tuned in

Conway Springs (map)

Some months after Marvin Kibbe was blinded in a hunting accident in 1966, he was sitting at a table in a Topeka rehabilitation center, trying to cut up a clump of Play-Doh.

"That's what they used to teach you how to cut big pieces of meat, like steak," Kibbe said. "It was part of a class they called TDL — techniques of daily living. And I learned just about everything they taught, but I never did get the hang of cutting that gob of Play-Doh."

That's all right, though, because he does just fine with radios, scanners, tape recorders and telephones, and he knows his way around police headquarters. For 18 years, Kibbe has been the police dispatcher in Conway Springs.

"2-0-6, Conway one, 10-23 at the site of a vandalized car. . . . "

That's Kibbe on the radio, talking to one of the town's two patrolmen. There are four police employees in Conway — Chief Lance Andra, the two officers and Kibbe.

"The best thing about this job is it gets me out of the house all day," he said. "I'd probably be in the loony bin if I had to stay in the house."

When he returned home from the rehabilitation hospital after his accident, he did have to stay at home. And it did drive him crazy.

"During that period, when my wife was teaching, I think I played every tape in the world. I went around the house and tightened every loose screw or loose anything I could find."

He also played around with citizens band radios, and that's how he was discovered by the town's former police chief.

"He had seen all those antennas on top of my house, and he came by and said, 'Evidently, you know something about radios.' And I said, 'Oh, I don't know nothin' about nothin',' " Kibbe said.

"So he said, 'How'd you like to come work as a dispatcher?' And after that, I reported to work."

His workstation has all the equipment that any dispatcher would use — a tape recorder, several scanners, a radio microphone and two telephones. The only difference is Kibbe's "talking clock." Push the button, and a computerized voice says, "Nine thirty-two, ay-em."

Conway Springs is a sleepy little town about 30 miles southwest of Wichita. "But you'd be surprised at some of the cases we get involved in," Kibbe said. "It's just like a big city, only on a small scale."

The police dispatcher's desk is in a small office inside the Conway Springs Community Building, which doubles as a senior citizens' center. Kibbe said he likes visiting with the town's older residents, especially since, at 66, he's nearing retirement age himself.

But he's not thinking about quitting.

"I enjoy meeting with the people, and I enjoy getting on the ol' radio and talking to somebody," Kibbe said. "You're just like an old fire-horse. You hear the whistle blow, and you just want to know what the heck is going on."

Many times, alarms turn out to be nothing much at all — someone burning trash, a dog running loose, a fender bender. But when major emergencies happen, townspeople know they can rely on Kibbe.

"It's just like a football game," he said. "These guys are throwing me the ball, and I'm going to see how far I can go with it."

SNAPSHOT BIOGRAPHY

Marvin Kibbe was born April 11, 1928, in Conway Springs. He graduated from Conway Springs High School in 1946 and married his wife, Beverly, on July 26, 1953. He has three children and 13 grandchildren. Years in Kansas: 66.

Marvin Kibbe coordinates Conway Springs police and EMS.

Police dispatcher Marvin Kibbe often rides along with the officer on duty at the beginning of the day.

Max Kirkes specializes in cowboy wood carvings — boots, ropes, hats and the like. "I look forward to every day," he says.

Whittling Away Time

Max Kirkes is carving out a pleasant existence

Wichita

Max Kirkes left the classroom for the back room, a little wood shop beside his home, where a man can get lost in his work.

"If I'm working on something new, I can stay up all night long just to see what it's going to look like," he said.

Kirkes worked for 35 years as a teacher in Kansas. Now, in retirement, he whittles away time, using his hands, his collection of carving knives and his imagination to carve little sculptures out of wood. His work is known throughout the area.

"It's relaxing, and time means nothing," he said. "If you were trying to make a living at this the way I do it, you'd starve."

But he's not trying to make a living. He's done that.

"The first day of school the year I retired, someone called me that afternoon and said, 'Don't you miss it?' And I said, 'Yeah, for about a twentieth of a second.'"

Kirkes smiled, rocking back and forth in his chair. A miniature wooden horse began to take shape in his hands, its head, mane and legs becoming more visible with each flick of his wrist. On the shelves of his workshop were about a dozen miniature cowboys, carved and painted, complete with razor stubble and holes in the knees of their blue jeans. Beside them was a box of little wooden shoes with upholstery-thread shoelaces.

After years of carving, Kirkes has developed a knack for sharpening knives, which he does with special grinders in one part of his shop. "People have sent me knives in the mail from as far away as New York and California, just asking if I'd sharpen them," he said. "I guess it's not easy to find someone who'll do them right."

Some might say that whittling is a lost art, gone the way of cowboys and steam engines and good storytelling. Whittling takes patience. It takes imagination. It takes a person who likes the simple things, like sitting by the wood stove, just thinking.

"I spend quite a bit of time by myself. Maybe you have to like yourself a lot to do that," Kirkes said. "But if someone comes by, that's OK, too."

Kirkes grew up on a farm in the Oklahoma hills. He had some horses and worked the land, and he still likes going to rodeos and watching old cowboy movies. His old saddle sits in his shop, not far from the rocking chair and wood stove.

And although he doesn't rope or ride anymore, one particular cowboy custom fits perfectly with his new, more relaxed lifestyle — cowboy poetry. On one chilly winter evening, Kirkes recited one of his favorite poems, about friendship:

Your friends are happy to see your success,
They're proud of your good side and forgive all the rest.
And that's not easy all the time,
Because sometimes we get crazy and seem to go blind.

And your friends might have to just take you on home,
Or remind you sometimes that you're not alone.
And ever so gently pull you back to the ground
When you think you can fly, and there's no one around.
A hug or a shake, whichever seems right
Is the high point of giving, and I'll tell you tonight,
All worldly riches and tributes of men
Can't hold a candle to the worth of a friend.

A sleepy black cat used to keep Kirkes company sometimes, but "he went a honky-tonkin' and never came back," he said. But when you're in the laid-back business of whittling, your best friend is yourself.

It's the life we all dream about at one time or another.

"I'm under no pressure at all. I do exactly what I want to do," Kirkes said. "I look forward to every day."

SNAPSHOT BIOGRAPHY

Max Kirkes was born Jan. 30, 1930, in Roff, Okla. He earned his bachelor's and master's degrees in education from East Central State University in Ada, Okla., and worked for 35 years as a teacher in Kansas. He and his wife, Donna Kirkes, were married July 6, 1963, in Cunningham. They have four sons. Years in Kansas: 37.

Max Kirkes carves one of his cowboys.

Martha Knudsen first photographs barns, then bases her detailed sketches on the multiple detail shots she has taken.

Barn Lover

Martha Knudsen used to play in them; now she re-creates them

Newton

When Martha Knudsen was growing up in northeast Kansas, her family and friends always knew where to find her — in the barn.

She'd spend hours there — in her own family's barn or someone else's — jumping into piles of hay, reading or just watching the world outside, enjoying the fresh, natural smells of rural life. "Daydreaming, mostly," she says. "I don't really know what I did there. I just know I loved being inside barns. You could just stick me out there, and I was happy."

She grew up to become a dental hygienist, working inside antiseptic offices in Wichita and Newton, but her heart stayed in the country. So when she retired in 1986, she rediscovered the relaxed beauty of barns.

This time, though, she did it with pen and ink. For almost a decade, Knudsen has wandered the back roads of Kansas, looking for interesting barns, snapping pictures of them and returning to her rural Harvey County home to re-create them on paper.

Her work is part art, part history, preserving old barns that are other people's memories. She has produced four barn calendars — with a pen-and-ink drawing to illustrate each month — and a book of her sketches. Her work has been exhibited at the Newton Art Association, the Newton Public Library, Century II in Wichita and several county and state fairs.

"I ask relatives and friends if they've seen any unusual barns, and they send pictures or directions," she says. "Then I just take a day to go out looking."

She avoids highways, opting instead for the dirt roads of rural Kansas, where barns loom like skyscrapers on the horizon. She dodges mud puddles, tractors, dogs and cows to get up close to a barn.

Then she snaps pictures to use as a reference when she starts drawing.

She returns to her own farm outside Newton — named "The Red Barn Farm" in honor of the Knudsens' own beautiful landmark — to start the real work. From the pictures, she creates an outline of the barn in pencil and carefully re-creates each wooden board, window or pitched roof. If the barn door is open, it's open in her drawing. If there's a windmill out front, she draws the windmill. If there's an old-fashioned rooster weather vane on top of the barn — like one she found in Cheyenne County — she draws the rooster right down to his arched tail feathers.

"You never know where to start sometimes," she said. "Sometimes it's hard to tell on the windows, and since I like detail, I use a magnifying glass a lot."

Looking at the picture through her magnifying glass, Knudsen inspects each detail — limestone fences, wooden door fasteners or the shadows below a curved "hip joint" roof — and adds them to her sketch. Sometimes, though, if an old barn is weathered and crumbling, she refurbishes it on the page. This, she says, is the historic preservation part of her art.

Then, after practicing pen-and-ink shading on a photocopy of her pencil sketch, Knudsen completes the work and erases the pencil lines. She usually gives the original artwork to the barn's owner, as thanks for allowing her to add the barn to her collection. And with each completed sketch, she remembers the days she used to sit or play or wander or daydream in barns, and she hopes she gives the old buildings something back for the joy they continue to bring her.

"I've always said they'll have to drag me off the farm," she said. "I really love it out here."

Martha Knudsen works on a drawing in her home studio.

Home on the Range

Jane Koger's Homestead Ranch lets wannabe cowgirls learn the ropes

Matfield Green

Let me get this straight, a neighbor once asked Chase County rancher Jane Koger. People *pay* you to come and do your chores?

That's right, and they've never had so much fun.

Koger's 6,000-acre Homestead Ranch in Chase County, not far from Matfield Green, serves two purposes. It's a working cattle ranch, and it's also part of Prairie Women Adventures and Retreat, a program that lets wannabe cowgirls learn what a

Jane Koger's Homestead Ranch is a working cattle ranch.

home on the range really means.

"It's a lot of work," Koger said. "But I wouldn't ranch again without Prairie Women or a guest program."

Koger's for-women-only ranch attracts guests from all over the United States and other countries. It is a place where nature is the classroom, where women can learn the cattle business from the ground up or simply go for a quiet walk and enjoy the peaceful isolation of prairie life.

"I can show you a stack of letters I get from women who say, 'I always wanted to be a cowgirl. I always wanted to own a ranch.' And all we're trying to do is give them that opportunity," Koger said.

Often, the opportunity is more than they bargained for. As part of the program, which can be a three-day weekend or Monday-to-Friday stay, guests learn how to round up cattle, vaccinate and brand calves and check cows for pregnancy. Your average rancher might call those things chores; to Koger and her guests, they're lessons in life.

"When women come here, the things I want them to experience are internal for them as well, a sense of empowerment that they got to do something they didn't think they could do," she

said. "That could be branding a calf or driving a tractor, or it may be just petting a cow."

Koger wants women to have a better understanding of ranch life, but also to appreciate the part animals play in our lives.

"One of the comments that I hear a lot, that means a lot to me, is, 'Jane, I've seen cows all my life, and I drive by them on my way to work. But they'll never look the same.' And then I know that something's happened."

It's not hard for something to happen to a person, looking at the scenic Flint Hills of Chase County. This place is far from the traffic and noise of the city, sheltered instead by rolling prairie and that big Kansas sky. Koger knows firsthand what that sort of tranquillity can do.

"The retreat part is that I'd like for them to be able to walk down on one of these Flint Hills and just get back in touch with themselves."

Koger's goal of empowering women and helping people appreciate the beauty of the prairie transcends her ranch and its guest program. In 1994 she played host to "Symphony on the Prairie," a 90-minute outdoor concert performed by a 60-piece orchestra of women. She said it was her gift to her neighbors, the 3,000 or so residents of Chase County.

Koger, a fourth-generation resident of the county, said she has found her place. It is here, amid the grass and sky and warm smell of cattle.

"This should be against the law, to like what you're doing so well," she said.

"Sometimes I think we can actually grow down into the soil. It happens. . . . This is where I belong. I'd be here without Prairie Women. I'd be here without a ranch. This is where I belong."

Jane Koger enjoys the Flint Hills with her black Labrador, Traveler.

Following Her Bliss

Sharon Lawrence's stone turret takes her back to the Renaissance

Wichita

Sharon Lawrence signs her letters, "Follow your bliss."

And that's what she has done, building a Renaissance-style tower in her back yard, adjacent to one of Wichita's busiest streets and visible to thousands of motorists each day.

She has followed her bliss, creating something from another time and place. Something called "Stargate Hermitage."

"People have written me letters. Or they drive by to say, 'It's wonderful. It's inspirational. I just love to see it,' " Lawrence said. "Just a spot of beauty as they go by."

A member of the Society for Creative Anachronisms, Lawrence admires the Renaissance era, from the traditional dress to the unusual lifestyle. She has even chosen a medieval name for herself — Lady Kasimira Verena D'Arcy, which means "peacemaker and sacred wisdom." But the looming three-story stone turret in her back yard is her love. The project took more than four years to complete.

"I did a great deal of sacrificing and hard work to produce this dream. It not only had to be in my heart and mind, but I had to work extremely hard — willing to do that day and night — and hold that vision for four years."

Why is she dedicated to re-creating the Renaissance in her back yard? The answer may surprise you.

"Well, I think I lived then," she said. "It's a remembering. It's like I'm there. I'm home. Some folks will take exception to that, and some won't."

Some people don't understand it, and they have told her so.

"I just love them anyway and say, 'Oh, well.' Just look at the flowers. You don't have to understand it. Take what you can love, and forget the rest.

"I just try to blend in the best I can. Like in that movie, 'Sister Act,' all the nuns are running around and one says, 'Try to blend in.' I love that line," Lawrence said, laughing. "I'm trying to blend in. I can't, really, but I try."

The name "Stargate" symbolizes a gateway from the past to the future, Lawrence said. And this project she has chosen — more accurately, she said, it has chosen her — is a way of "trying to make the world a little better in some way."

Children have toured the tower, troubled adolescents have found solitude there, and Lawrence has

even offered free access to the Wichita Children's Home and the Make a Wish Foundation. Through it, she hopes to give children a somewhat unusual lesson in history.

"When I was in high school, history was duller than toast. I didn't care at all," she said. "But I came to care because I want to know where we as a people and a planet have been and where we are going."

The people driving past her tower near Hillside and Kellogg in Wichita are going about 50 miles an hour. But even at that speed, amid the fast pace of modern life, Lawrence's personal retreat is noticed. Why build so close to the traffic?

"I just consider it like a roaring, raging river, because it's just noise all the time," she said.

In December 1993, she opened her back yard and the tower to the public. Curious visitors drank steamy hot cider, lighted luminaries that symbolized prayers for peace and enjoyed the greatest view of Kellogg in the whole city.

"You have to bloom where you're planted," she said. "I live here, so I built it here. Then I got to thinking, I can create all this beauty and all these people can enjoy it."

Sharon Lawrence on the ground floor of Stargate Hermitage.

SNAPSHOT BIOGRAPHY

Sharon Sue Lawrence was born Nov. 8, 1941, in Eureka. She graduated from high school in Camdenton, Mo., and attended the Dr. Vodder School of Manual Lymph Drainage in Walchsee, Austria, where she was certified in that popular European form of physical therapy. She and her husband, Sheldon, were married Jan. 18, 1964, in Wichita. They have two children. Years in Kansas: 42.

Excalibur awaits King Arthur in the garden beside Sharon Lawrence's Stargate Hermitage.

Mae Lenway says her ability to whistle is a gift from God. Husband Boyd likes listening to her as he works.

The Skiddy Whistler

Mae Lenway keeps the tunes coming and husband Boyd keeps listening

Skiddy

If you've ever wondered what keeps people happy, what keeps them going after their careers are done, their children gone, their town all but vanished, just listen to Mae Lenway.

"What tune do you want to hear?" she asked, sitting down at her kitchen table. "Do you have a favorite old-timey song?"

A strong breeze blew across the kitchen window and skipped across the overgrown grasses in the pastures outside, where clouds dotted the blue Kansas sky like dollops of whipped cream. Somehow, "Summertime (And the Livin' Is Easy)" seemed appropriate.

"I think I know that one," she said. "Let me get a glass of water."

By all means, wet your whistle. You see, they call Mae Lenway "the Skiddy whistler." About 20 years ago, as she was walking down the streets of the almost-forgotten Morris County town, she took a deep breath, pursed her lips and surprised herself.

"When I was a teenager, I couldn't whistle a note. Then all of a sudden, out of the clear blue sky, I started whistling," she said. "It's a gift from God. It really is."

This is no ordinary whistling. Imagine a combination of Andy Griffith and Boston Pops, with a hearty dose of early-morning songbird. It is a symphony of sound.

"I can't explain it really," she said. "I just do it."

For the past 15 years, she has taken her show on the road, performing at schools, churches and nursing homes in more than 65 Kansas communities. All she needs is her Billy Vaughn records, a glass of water and a captive audience. Her favorite tune is "Tumbling Tumbleweed"; her most requested one, particularly at retirement centers, is "Shine On Harvest Moon."

"I start whistling, and people start nodding their heads or humming along," she said. "Sometimes I shake things up with 'Sweet Georgia Brown.' "

As she whistled "Summertime," the notes climbed and fell, skipping like the breeze outside her window. At times, the melody was more of a warble, with sharp trills that sounded like robins in the spring.

Listening from the other room was Mae's husband, Boyd. He once served in the U.S. Army cavalry at Fort Riley, so an entire wall of their garage, Boyd's office, is covered with old bits, bridles and stirrups. Upstairs, another room is full of coffee cups, patches, plaques and uniforms — mementos of Boyd's 60 years of service to the Boy Scouts of America.

He likes listening to Mae's special music while he rummages through the past.

"She'll start whistling, and I just listen to her and keep on working, you know?" he said. "If I get tired of it, I just go downstairs, but you can still listen to it."

The Lenways' home is the old Standard Oil station and garage in downtown Skiddy. It closed in the early 1950s, but the trademark red, white and blue sign remains out front as a reminder of how vital the town used to be.

"This was quite a place once," Boyd Lenway said, gazing out at the nearly deserted roads. "We had a 43-room motel, a dry goods store, a post office, three churches, a beer joint, a creamery, a locker plant, a school and three stores. After the school quit in '53, everything kind of started closing up.

"We stayed, though. We like it here."

Who wouldn't? All you really need, as Mae Lenway will tell you, is a song in your heart.

And a glass of water.

SNAPSHOT BIOGRAPHY

Mae Lenway was born May 14, 1920, in Cedar Rapids, Iowa. She and her husband, Boyd, who is from Faribault, Minn., met at a roller-skating rink in Cedar Rapids when both were teenagers. The couple married July 1, 1941, in Junction City. Boyd served in the U.S. Army during World War II and the Korean War, and the Lenways lived in several cities during his military career. They also lived 20 years in California, where Boyd worked for the U.S. Forest Service. The Lenways moved to Skiddy in 1976. Years in Kansas: 22.

Sculpting His Opinions

M.T. Liggett lets his "political statement totem poles" speak for him

Go ahead, call M.T. Liggett a kook.

You wouldn't be the first. Many a soul, both resident and tourist, has driven by Liggett's pasture just west of Mullinville and thought, "What kind of person would do this?" Some have stopped to take pictures of the crude metal sculptures, proof that pioneer ingenuity and eccentricity — not to mention freedom of expression — still exist on the wide-open countryside of western Kansas.

"A lot of people go through their whole lives and never make a mark," Liggett said. "Very few people in this world ever had an original idea, but I did. So if they want to call me crazy, go ahead. I don't care."

A retired soldier and part-time breeder of Brahman bulls, Liggett now spends his spare time crafting what he describes as "political statement totem poles." They are something between art and commentary, oversize sculptures fashioned out of scrap metal and Liggett's own brash opinions, and they line the roadway on U.S. 154.

There's the one about President Clinton — a piece of metal that says "Dump the hicks in ninety-six," with the faces of "Slick Willie" and "Prince Albert" smiling like jack-o'-lanterns amid whirligigs that spin in the breeze.

There's the one about Clinton's health-care plan — "4012 pages of liberal vomit," according to Liggett's artwork. A score of other sculptures take aim at Hillary Rodham Clinton, Ross Perot, the Kiowa County Commission, the Mullinville City Council, Lorena Bobbitt, various local citizens and the federal officials who stormed the Branch Davidian compound in Waco, Texas.

The messages range from innocent to obscene,

but Liggett's point is always the same:

"I'm trying to get the American people to wise up to what our political system is doing to us," he said. "The whole thing this is, is to get people to stop and think."

Liggett's hobby began innocently enough. In an attempt to protect one of his favorite horses from evil elements, he fashioned two gargoyles out of farm implement discs and erected them near the pasture. They seemed to work fine, he said, and then he sold the horse.

Since then, Liggett has expressed his political opinions with discs and other scrap pieces of metal that he shapes with a cutting torch and welds together. He adds written messages — sometimes in foreign languages such as Latin, Spanish and French, and sometimes in such obscure English that Liggett has to translate them for you, anyway.

When a Dodge City official compared illegal aliens to cockroaches, saying that when you sprayed one place, they'd turn up someplace else, Liggett was prompted into action. He crafted a totem pole with the politician's name, the phrases "ethnic cleansing" and "gestapo," and, of course, a cockroach.

"She wasn't too pleased when she heard about this one," Liggett said.

"But you know what I say: You can't go through this world thinking about what people think of you or patterning your life around somebody else. If

you're gonna worry about what everybody thinks, it's time to call Jack Kevorkian."

Liggett's totem poles have made him somewhat of an outcast around Mullinville.

"They don't like me too much, that's for sure," he said. "But when you think something, you've got to say it. That's what's wrong with our world today —

SNAPSHOT BIOGRAPHY

M.T. Liggett was born Dec. 28, 1930, in Mullinville. He earned his associate degree from Dodge City Junior College and studied political science, history and criminal justice at Fort Hays State University and the University of Nevada at Las Vegas. He also attended West Texas State University. He served nine years in the U.S. Navy and 15 years in the Army before retiring in his hometown. He has been married six times but is currently unmarried. He has five children. Years in Kansas: 40.

not enough people say what they really think."

And lest you think Liggett prefers to stay outside the political arena, he did run for a spot on the school board recently. The result? "Record low," he said, chuckling.

But he's not going to stop making his totem poles and advertising his political opinions to the world. Eventually, he hopes to fill a 27-acre pasture just east of town, and he's got plenty of land left after that.

So go ahead, call him a kook. Just do him a favor, and say it like you mean it.

M.T. Liggett spends his spare time crafting what he calls "political statement totem poles."

Fighting Cultural Bias

Charles and Vicki Little Coyote do so by teaching Indian ways

Medicine Lodge

When a vicious spring wind howls and bends the trees outside their home, Charles and Vicki Little Coyote aren't afraid.

"No, this storm is gonna be good," Vicki said, walking toward the kitchen to prepare herself a fresh cup of coffee. "Charlie's gonna split it, so it will go around us. It's the Indian way."

Charles Little Coyote is a descendant of Black Kettle.

The Little Coyotes want to calm the prejudice that surrounds Indian people and their culture, and they do it by teaching Indian ways to youngsters and adults of all races and backgrounds.

"There are some people that are prejudiced against the Indian. Why, I don't know," said Charles, a man with dark, leathery skin. He is a direct descendent of the great Cheyenne Indian chief, Black Kettle.

"We've been called everything from witches to warlocks to good people," Vicki added.

"Indians got feelings like everybody else," Charles continued. "When I was in the war, I cried like everybody else. But it's kind of hard when someone's talking you down."

"As long as they talk about us," Vicki said, "they're leaving someone else alone."

That, too, is the Indian way. Courtesy and sensitivity toward others. Leave the criticism with us, Vicki says, and we'll handle it. We'll explain our ways and hope they understand.

The Little Coyotes regularly attend festivals and powwows and speak to schoolchildren about the Cheyenne culture and traditions. They hope that increasing the awareness of Native American culture will bridge the ever-increasing gap between cultures.

"What we always tell them is, 'We're going to teach you everything that you didn't learn in movies or books,' " said Vicki, who traces her lineage back to Kit Carson. "So much of that is wrong."

Outside their home in Medicine Lodge, the couple sometimes set up camp and sleep outside. Charles

often is host of "sweat lodge" and "sundance" ceremonies, where the air is filled with Indian dancing and the sound of Charles' voice singing ancient songs passed down to him from his ancestors.

What they find now, though, is that few American Indians even know their own roots. Throughout America today, the soft, quiet ways of the Indian have been replaced by violence.

"I wonder about these big cities. I watch TV, these drive-by shootings — why? Why? Why do people want to do that?" Charles said. "Nowadays to me, it's greed. Too many people are greedy, and it's not supposed to be that way."

Vicki Little Coyote is known as a "master beadswoman," and she hand-sews the beads on all of the couple's traditional Indian costumes. Charles is one of the chiefs of the Southern Cheyenne tribe and oversees tribal ceremonies.

At a recent festival to celebrate the Santa Fe Trail and its historic path through Kansas, the Little Coyotes spoke about Indian culture and traditions. Charles ended his lesson with a farewell spoken in his native Cheyenne language:

"We are happy to be here to tell you our culture, the Cheyenne culture. And someday, somewhere, we will see each other again."

SNAPSHOT BIOGRAPHY

Charles Little Coyote was born Oct. 26, 1926, in Fonda, Okla. He is a full-blooded Southern Cheyenne descended from Chief Black Kettle. Vicki Little Coyote was born April 18, 1939, in Manhattan. The couple married Nov. 18, 1988, in Fonda. They have 16 children, including four daughters and four sons adopted through Indian tradition. Years in Kansas: Charles 40, Vicki 55.

Vicki and Charles Little Coyote teach Indian ways to youngsters and adults of all races and backgrounds.

85

Turning Trash Into Treasure

Patsy Magelssen finds joy in making gifts for those in need

McPherson

At the end of your conversation with Patsy Magelssen, she finds a scrap piece of paper and makes you promise to keep it in your wallet. On it, she writes her name, two telephone numbers and this, in capital letters: "ANYTHING FREE."

"If you hear about anything — leftover material, toys, yarn, fiber-fill, anything — you let me know," she said, her eyes as round as those on the stuffed doll behind her. "We'll find something to do with it, I can tell you that.'

Magelssen turns trash to treasure. In a room on the third floor of Bank IV in downtown McPherson, she collects boxes full of other people's junk and assembles dolls, stuffed animals, quilts, clothes, hand puppets, pillows, bibs, duffel bags and just about anything else you can imagine. This is headquarters for Trash to Treasure, a non-profit group that keeps Magelssen busier than Santa Claus.

SNAPSHOT BIOGRAPHY

Patsy Ann Magelssen was born March 19, 1940, in Minneapolis, Minn. She and her husband, Luther, married on April 11, 1959, and have three children. They lived in several cities in Minnesota before moving to McPherson in 1992. Years in Kansas: 2.

"Come over here," she said, "and I'll show you what we've got so far."

Magelssen first started Trash to Treasure in the basement of her house in Owatonna, Minn. She wanted to do something to honor her late mother, who taught her the phrase, "One man's trash is another man's treasure." So, with the 1959 Singer sewing machine her mother gave her as a graduation gift, Magelssen began sewing stuffed dolls and Humpty Dumptys and giving them away to needy children at Christmas.

Before long, her project outgrew her family's basement, and she started working out of a Lutheran church in Owatonna. When churchgoers and other friends of Magelssen's saw what she was doing, they started bringing materials and volunteering their time to make toys and other gifts.

"The more I talked about it, the more people were willing to help," she said. "Before you knew it, we were having a once-a-week get-together. Then I started going around to companies and asking for their leftovers."

From a company in St. Cloud that produces marine life jackets, Magelssen scored pieces of heavy nylon material, and — presto! — she started making duffel bags. Yarn manufacturers contributed scrap or irregular yarn, which Magelssen used for doll hair and various other toys. And friends kept bringing in their scrap material, clothes, toys and everything else from attics and closets.

The Magelssens moved to McPherson in 1992, when Patsy's husband, Luther, got a job as president of the city's Bank IV branch. And shortly after arriving, Patsy Magelssen was hard at work again, finding materials and rounding up volunteers. That year, Trash to Treasure made 2,100 gifts — at a total cost of less than $500 — and distributed them to rescue missions, homeless shelters and children's homes across Kansas.

Why does she do it?

"You know, that is the worst question in the whole world. . . . I don't know. It's got to be a higher power that gave me the ability to create things and the love to give it away."

A whole room at Trash to Treasure headquarters is filled with materials — bits of cloth, yarn and other donations — all organized and carefully labeled in cardboard boxes that reach from floor to ceiling. The rest of the office is saved for finished products, which, by November, cover every inch of the floor and even hang from the ceilings. In 1993 volunteers made more than 3,000 gifts and distributed them to about 25 organizations.

The McPherson County Sheriff's Department got dolls and other toys to keep in squad cars for youngsters involved in traffic accidents. Residents of a nursing home in Canton got "wheelchair bags" filled with goodies. Patients at a local Veterans Administration hospital got health-care bags filled with shampoo, soap, lotion and other supplies. And a church mission in Africa will distribute handmade skirts to natives and bags of washcloths and bandages to medical teams.

For her work, Magelssen was honored as a Point of Light by former President Bush and received the 1993 Volunteer Action Award from President Clinton. But for Magelssen, the greatest award is in the giving.

"Whenever we make something, it goes out with a simple tag that just says, 'I love you. Santa,' " she said. "Because I think love is what it's all about, and that's the greatest message of all."

Opposite: Patsy Magelssen's enthusiasm is contagious and is at the heart of her service organization, Trash to Treasure.

Gary Mason was born June 17, 1936, in Coffeyville. He moved as a youngster to Independence and graduated from Independence High School. He attended Emporia State University, where he earned his bachelor's degree in business and his master's in education. He taught photojournalism at the University of Kansas for several years. He and his wife, Sarah, were married Aug. 17, 1963, in Emporia. Years in Kansas: 58.

After spending time working with Mother Teresa in India, Gary Mason moved to Emporia and became director of the Emporia Senior Center.

Giving Something Back

Gary Mason is building bridges with his work at the Emporia Senior Center

Emporia

When Gary Mason went to Calcutta, India, as a volunteer to work with Mother Teresa, he felt as if he'd been born again.

In America, his life, like most other American lives, had revolved around things — buying things, owning things, wanting more things. In Calcutta, he was humbled.

He was a photojournalist and teacher when he went to India, and he brought home many photographs of Mother Teresa helping the poor. But his most vivid memories couldn't be captured on film.

"I look back on it, and I was just with God," he said. "I stopped being a photojournalist when I went there. . . . There were so many times when I felt so uncomfortable even taking a picture of her, that I didn't."

Today, Mason is director of the Emporia Senior Center, where he helps serve up to 400 meals a day to the city's elderly, listens to their stories and songs, and offers many hugs.

"It's a real joy," he said. "This is a hugging place."

Mason spent three months in Calcutta in 1988 and three more months there in 1989. His job was to bathe the dying. He described one of many memorable, tragic experiences:

"Then I would start to rub the temples of the head, so I moved around to do that, and he was stone cold. But the place that I'd been rubbing on his back was still warm."

Most people would be depressed from such experiences and never want to return. Mason, on the other hand, felt his work in helping some of the world's poorest people was "giving something back to God," and he wants to do it again.

"It stays with me every day," he said. "I've never forgotten. I must go back."

And he wishes everyone could see firsthand the squalor and poverty in Calcutta. Maybe then, he said, Americans would realize how blessed we are.

"They have nothing. They just exist," he said. "I wish Americans would open up their eyes and see the poor, the hungry, and quit being so materialistic. Because truly, everything belongs to God, and he will take it away from you.

"It's all a very humbling experience for an American, because here, even the poor are still rich. The poor in Calcutta, they have absolutely nothing."

As part of his effort to give something back, Mason has made one of his portraits of Mother Teresa into a poster, and he wants to distribute copies to the more than 500 homes in the world where sisters like Mother Teresa are helping the poor.

"A lot of people don't realize the kind of work the Mother does, and one of these days, she is going to die," he said. "I just want to make sure she is remembered."

During his short time in Calcutta, Mason dealt in death. Now, at the Emporia Senior Center, he enjoys life. He came to Emporia in 1993 to care for his 93-year-old mother-in-law. He and his wife left their home in Baldwin, just outside Lawrence, and he gave up a free-lance photography career there.

He applied for the director's job at the Senior Center because, he said, "I just saw it as a continuation of the kind of work I want to do for the rest of my life."

Recently, he picked up his camera again to work on a collection of portraits of the elderly, as well as bits of advice that the elderly would give to young people. He hopes the book, whenever it is completed, will "build a bridge between the young and old."

Much the way Mason builds bridges with his work at the senior center.

"A lot of people don't like to come here, because they think this is a place for old people or poor people," he said. "It isn't either one. These people are not old, and they're certainly rich, very rich. God has given them lots of good things."

God has blessed Mason with good things, too, he says.

"My job here is just the continuation of a beautiful life," he said. "They say that whatever you give, you get back twice, and I believe that."

Gary Mason hugs Margaret Queen, an active member of the Emporia Senior Center.

Water Witcher

Believe what you like, but Carl McKee says he can find water

Some things you can't explain. Some things, like some people, you either believe or you don't.

Take ol' Carl McKee.

Ol' Carl has a hobby, see — some might even call it a gift — and you either believe it or you don't. It's called "water witching," or just "witchin'," and it's a practice as old as the Kansas prairie.

The explanation, such as it is, goes like this: A water witcher, such as Carl McKee, takes a Y-shaped stick in his hands and walks with the bottom branch of the "Y" pointing straight toward the sky. At times, the branch will pull and flip in his hand, and the bottom branch will point straight toward the ground, toward the place where, if you were to dig a well, you'd eventually hit water.

That's how it works. McKee, a heavyset man in blue denim overalls, has been doing it since 1966.

"Now I'll see how deep the water is here," he said, standing over the spot where his magic stick told him water would be. "Is it 10 foot? Is it 20 foot? Is it 30 foot? Is it 40 foot? It's starting to pull. Is it 50 foot?"

Flip.

"There, it goes down."

McKee can tell you not only the location of an underground vein of water and how deep it is, but also the rate of flow.

"Is it five gallons per minute? Six gallons? Seven gallons? . . . Sixteen gallons per minute?"

Flip.

"I see you shaking your head."

More than a few spectators of this age-old hobby have been known to shake their heads in disbelief. It can't work, they say. Carl McKee's no geologist, and a forked stick is hardly modern technology. And there's no scientific evidence to support water witching, after all. At best, it's coincidence; at worst, a good show.

"I know what they're going to think," said McKee. After working as a mechanic, farmer, cattleman and landscaper, he has retired. But even in retirement, he keeps on witching.

"They'll say that the man's crazy, that it can't be. And I can't explain it. . . . It is kind of a weird sensation when you feel that stick twist in your hand like that."

How accurate is McKee? He said that out of 186 wells he has "witched," or predicted, since he began, he has been nearly 100 percent right. But if you choose to believe modern science and laugh off witching, McKee said, go right ahead.

"Oh, it don't bother me in the least. I just ignore it, make fun of it. You've got to have a little fun out of life, and this is what I try to do.

"As old as I'm getting, you've got to have a little fun."

So believe it or not. It doesn't much matter to Carl McKee. He just keeps on walking, with that magic stick pointing to the clouds.

Carl McKee asks his water witching branch, "How deep is the water?"

SNAPSHOT BIOGRAPHY

Carl McKee was born May 4, 1921, in Wellington. He graduated from high school in 1939 and married his wife, Vada, in January 1950. Years in Kansas: 73.

Carl McKee "witches" for water near his home in Wellington.

Making Modern Heirlooms

Mary Ellen McKee wants the christening gowns she makes to last

Salina

From generation to generation, families share common threads. For some, one of the most precious is a christening gown designed and sewn by Mary Ellen McKee.

McKee wants to bring back a Victorian tradition, creating heirloom-quality christening gowns with fine lace and intricate embroidery that stand the test of time. She calls them "modern heirlooms."

"I would like to see these gowns around for 200 to 250 years from now. Long after I'm gone," she said.

Working in the loft of her Salina home, McKee stitches each piece of silk batiste, cotton, organza or linen, her fingers gently guiding the delicate fabric through the machine. Her mother taught her to sew on an old-fashioned trundle, and she has been doing it ever since.

She began sewing christening gowns in 1988. After raising seven children and sewing gowns for 15 grandchildren, she thought it was time to share her work with others.

"It's something I always wanted to do, because a christening gown is such a special thing," she said. "The ones you see in stores, they're nice, but they seem so simple and plain and unpersonalized."

Her favorite part of sewing her own gowns is seeing infants draped in her creations, their faces as pure and angelic as the white lace.

"I just love it, because I love children. I love babies," McKee said. "It's sort of like a person who loves horses, you know, how that person will learn everything they can about horses, and just memorize the horse's body?

"Well, I know every nook and cranny on those babies. Just sitting here, I could draw the face of a child."

Consequently, McKee doesn't need to use store-bought patterns when she sews. Working from a basic style that fits almost any infant, she embellishes each gown with special details — puffy sleeves, tucks, perhaps a bit of lace from a grandmother's wedding dress — to make it a one-of-a-kind work of art. Some of the christening gowns can be converted into Holy Communion dresses, and then, when the girl becomes an adult, into a dress for the flower girl.

"That's the best thing of all, that a christening gown can be used again for all those special days," she said.

Some of McKee's works have received national attention. She sent christening gowns to Deborah Norville and Maria Shriver, former hosts of "Today" on NBC, and to Katie Couric, the show's current host. Couric sent McKee a letter of thanks, with a picture of her newborn daughter wearing the gown.

McKee admits it was something of a publicity stunt, sending baby clothes to big-name television stars, but it was fun.

"When all those gals were turning up pregnant, I thought, why not do something crazy?" she said. For the first daughter of Shriver and Arnold Schwarzenegger, McKee made an organza gown covered with embroidery; for Couric's little girl, an old-fashioned cotton batiste gown with puffy sleeves and a detachable bonnet.

Each year, McKee donates a few gowns to local hospitals, where they are auctioned off for charity. She would like to one day make custom-made gowns for Neiman-Marcus or another fine clothier.

For now, though, it is enough to see the joy her gowns bring to her Kansas customers, especially the young ones. She remembers one particular youngster on her way to her first Holy Communion, wearing one of McKee's creations.

"It was just wonderful. A little girl was just prancing around and swirling," McKee said. "It was just a fun thing to watch. . . . There's a lot of peace and serenity in what I'm doing."

Mary Ellen McKee creates christening gowns with fine lace and intricate embroidery.

SNAPSHOT BIOGRAPHY

Mary Ellen McKee was born June 10, 1936, in Adams Center, N.Y. She married Quentin McKee on March 8, 1952. She attended two and a half years of college at three Kansas universities — Marymount College in Salina, Kansas State University and the University of Kansas. She and her husband have seven children and 15 grandchildren. Years in Kansas: 50.

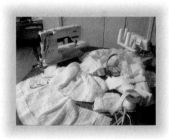

Mary Ellen McKee dresses a doll to display one of her christening gowns.

The House That Rosa Built

Rosa Molina's vision helped La Familia Multicultural Center become a reality

Derby

There's a building at 841 W. 21st Street in Wichita, where people of all ages come together to eat, play, talk with each other, even get a ride to the doctor's office.

You could call it the house that Rosa Molina built.

It is La Familia Multicultural Center, formerly the Hispanic Senior Shepherd Center, and it exists largely because Molina dreamed that it could.

"I'm not a talker," she said. "I'm not one of those people who complain and complain and complain and don't do anything about it. I'm a doer. I want to see results."

Rosa Molina says that she's a doer.

The results, in this case, came after years of hard work. Molina, who once served in a U.S. Army medical battalion and then worked as a nurse at HCA Wesley Medical Center in Wichita, became director of a newly formed Hispanic senior center in 1989, while on a voluntary leave of absence from the hospital.

At first, her office was an elementary-school classroom, with miniature desks and chairs and a slippery tile floor. Her entire budget was spent just getting a telephone line installed.

After several months, she moved to a tiny storefront on East 21st Street. "It was a dump," she said. "But I transformed that place. I got together everyone I knew, and we cleaned it up." In June 1990, the Hispanic Senior Shepherd Center had its first open house.

"The response was wonderful," Molina said. "There is so much need in this community — not just for the elderly, but for everybody in general. These people were getting services that never existed before, and they were so grateful."

Molina, who was 18 when she moved from her native Ecuador to the United States, knows the struggles Hispanic people can face in America. Almost two-thirds of her clients at the senior center could not speak English, and they didn't know where to go to learn. The center began offering English classes, and volunteer translators helped clients get to doctor's appointments, fill their prescriptions, apply for public assistance or just get a ride to the grocery store.

"This job was so demanding, and I just wanted to do so much for people," Molina said. "How can you turn anyone away? I couldn't."

And she didn't. She expanded the senior programs to include anyone over age 55, and she added more programs to help children and young families. Whatever money she could muster from government grants, she used to expand the center's services.

Some days she spent hours driving clients around town to appointments or helping them read letters. Other times, she worked the phones, trying to find jobs for unemployed Hispanics.

"Little by little, the word just spread through the community," she said. "People would come by and say, 'Look at my new grandchild,' or 'This is my son or daughter, and they have a problem. Can you help them out?' It just grew and grew."

In 1993 the center moved to its current location on West 21st, in the heart of the city's predominantly Hispanic neighborhood. A representative for the state Department on Aging has an office in the new center, and officials plan to spend $100,000 in Community Development Block Grant funds to expand the parking lot, add lighting and build a courtyard behind the center.

Seeing so many of her dreams for the center become reality, Molina retired from her position in May to spend more time with her family. Even so, she said, the vision continues.

"I want this to have all the services that anybody could need — a one-stop shop," she said. "Because this is not my building. This is everybody's building."

Rosa Molina in a meeting at the
La Familia Multicultural Center.

SNAPSHOT BIOGRAPHY

Rosa Molina was born Dec. 12, 1953, in Guayaquil, Ecuador. She moved with her parents to Yonkers, N.Y., in 1971. She and her husband, Wilson Molina, were married April 6, 1974, in Mount Vernon, N.Y. Shortly after their wedding, the couple joined the U.S. Army and were stationed at the 1st Medical Battalion at Fort Riley. After leaving the Army in 1977, the Molinas moved to Wichita, where Rosa earned a bachelor of arts degree in liberal arts and a bachelor of science in nursing from Wichita State University. They have three children. Years in Kansas: 18.

SNAPSHOT BIOGRAPHY

Charles Porubsky was born Oct. 24, 1922, in Topeka. He graduated from high school in Topeka and served several years in the U.S. Army during World War II. He and his wife, Lydia, were married Feb. 22, 1949. They have five children. Years in Kansas: 71.

Charles Porubsky's chili recipe is from his mother, the late Catherine Porubsky.

A Lot of Chili
Charles Porubsky serves that and more in his Topeka sandwich shop

Topeka

Some folks have said that Charles Porubsky's little sandwich shop is on the wrong side of the tracks. Several times a day, every day, a slow-moving train cuts off the road leading to the parking lot, and it makes a heck of a noise.

But when that train passes through Topeka on a cold day in January, when the big pots of homemade chili are bubbling and popping on Porubsky's stove and Charlie's wife, Lydia, is serving up hot ham-and-cheese sandwiches, it's the *other* side of the tracks that you don't want to be on.

Porubsky's, a combination neighborhood grocery, tavern and deli, is a Capital City tradition. All kinds of people gather there, from legislators and law students to blue-collar folks and men in bib overalls. The famous chili and down-home atmosphere calls them all.

The Porubskys started out in the grocery business in 1947, when Charles and his family took over a store in what was then a German-Russian neighborhood. Then big supermarkets began replacing little groceries, so in 1952, after their store was washed away in a flood, the Porubskys decided to rebuild and add a sandwich shop and tavern on the side.

The chili recipe is from the late Catherine Porubsky, Charlie's mother. So, exactly how many bowls has Porubsky served in 42 years?

"Oh, I don't have any idea," he said. "A week ago Thursday, when it rained and it was cold, we went through 50, 55, 58 gallons of chili in three hours. That's a lot of chili."

A lot of chili, and a lot of work. Charlie Porubsky knows it, but he never complains. He arrives at the restaurant about 8 a.m. and takes off around, well, we'll let him tell you.

"Last night it was 11:30."

At night?

"Eleven-thirty."

How do you do it?

"Easy."

How?

"I don't know how," he said, smiling and shrugging. "I just do it."

Porubsky's decor is as understated as its menu — a few booths, two tables, several barstools and a bar. The walls are decorated with photographs signed by well-known Kansas politicians, including governors John Carlin, Bob Bennett, Bob Docking and Joan Finney. Against one wall is a rack full of candy bars and bags of peanuts, and scattered through the place are the requisite bottles of mustard, ketchup and hot pepper sauce.

Although chili might be Porubsky's most famous entree, his high-stacked cold-cut sandwiches also have a loyal following, especially in the summertime.

And then there are those hot pickles. What's in those things, anyway? "Special spices," Porubsky said, and kept on making sandwiches.

"One turkey on wheat!"

"Who had the corned beef?"

Charles Porubsky waits on customers in the grocery part of his grocery/sandwich shop/tavern in Topeka.

"Four chilis!"

As the sign in the tavern says, "Good chili ain't jist fer breakfast anymore." At Porubsky's, the chili is one sign that in today's high-tech, fast-moving society, some things just can't be improved. Like good service.

"I think I know everybody in here, and they all know me."

A good family.

"It's like a home atmosphere out here, you know. Everybody's buddy-buddy."

And good chili.

"Sorry, I gotta go wait on this guy. . . . Chili? Chili!"

If the Shoe Fits . . .

Ann Quirk will collect it; she has thousands of them

Wellington

This shoe collection is made for gawking.

Ann Quirk's modest house along Wellington's main thoroughfare is filled with collectible ceramic and porcelain shoes — and just about anything else related to footwear.

Over 35 years, Quirk has collected more than 10,000 shoe items — shoe pictures, shoe towels, shoe magnets on the refrigerator, shoe-shaped thimbles, shoe key chains, shoe lamps, shoe clocks,

Ann Quirk's collection includes anything with shoes on it — postcards, scarves, plates and more.

and shelves upon shelves of dainty porcelain shoes.

"Actually, my collection is utterly useless, mainly because you only collect one — you never buy them in pairs — and you can't wear them," she said.

Nevertheless, Quirk can't seem to stop collecting shoes. Whenever she has a spare day or weekend, she browses through antique stores and flea markets to look for pieces she hasn't seen before. It's getting more and more difficult.

"It's very seldom anymore that I see something I don't already have," she said. "When you've been collecting for 35 years, you've kinda seen it all."

Quirk started collecting shoes after her grandmother gave her a shoe knickknack about the size of an apple — a "granny boot" style shoe made of white porcelain with gold-colored trim. She liked it, but it looked so lonely on her shelf.

"I just thought, that would be kind of a neat thing to collect," she said. "Never in my wildest dreams did I think it would get this big."

Quirk's collection may seem odd, but she's not the only person in the world who collects shoes. In fact, finely crafted glass, porcelain and china shoes are big business for some of the world's most renowned manufacturers, and the items are valuable. Quirk's collection includes shoes made by Lenox, Royal Worchester and Dresden, as well as Delft, a famous pottery in Holland, and Royal

Bayreuth, a German company.

Her collection has earned Quirk the unofficial title of "Shoe Lady" in Wellington, and some of her best friends are fellow shoe collectors from other parts of the country. Libby Yalom, a Maryland woman who wrote the book "Shoes of Glass," a catalog-style bible for shoe collectors, knows Quirk well and has given her an autographed copy of her book.

"When I first started collecting, I didn't think anyone else did this," she said. "Then I heard that a lady in Amarillo, Texas, collected shoes, and we've been corresponding for years."

Quirk's collection includes shoes made from all types of materials — wax, coal, chocolate, iron, cast stone, and even, believe it or not, marshmallows. She also has shoe music boxes and toys, including a toy terrier dog that, when you wind him up, drags a boot in his mouth. At Christmas, she sets up three full-size Christmas trees filled with shoe ornaments.

Does she have a favorite?

"Oh, I have lots of favorites," she says, smiling. "I like all the ones with animals. And I like this one." She lifts a delicate shoe off one of her shelves. It is made of brightly colored stained glass, crafted by an artist in western Kansas. "I just saw this one and had to have it."

Maybe collecting is in her blood. She only recently began collecting giraffes — she thinks they're cute — and she already has more than 200.

"Some people might think it's crazy," she said. "But I like it. The longer I collect, the more fascinating it becomes."

A white glass slipper from the turn of the century started Ann Quirk on her collection. The slipper was originally owned by her grandmother.

Richard Ranney was born Sept. 20, 1928, in Council Bluffs, Iowa. He attended the University of Iowa. Peg Ranney was born July 31, 1927, in Guthrie, Okla. She has a bachelor's degree in communications from Oklahoma State University. Richard and Peg met while both were working in the tourism industry — he for Iowa, and she for Oklahoma. They were married Nov. 18, 1979, in Guthrie. They moved to Dodge City in 1981. Years in Kansas: 13.

Peg and Richard Ranney run the Dodge City, Ford and Bucklin Railroad.

Working on the Railroad

Richard and Peg Ranney's line is a work in progress

Dodge City

Peg Ranney coordinates meals in the dining car.

Dick and Peg Ranney never dreamed they'd be working on the railroad. But several years ago, after a Chicago company bought a stretch of the old Rock Island line that runs through Dodge City and announced plans to scrap the line, the Ranneys came to the rescue.

Dick Ranney was director of the Dodge City Convention & Visitors Bureau at the time. He recognized the potential for not only preserving a piece of history, but also making it available to everybody.

"We thought it was important. We felt the nostalgia was important, the opportunity for kids to enjoy the trains," he said. "Kids of all ages enjoy trains."

The Ranneys bought the railroad in 1989 and worked for more than a year to replace railroad ties, buy and renovate historic train cars and get the train running again.

Today, the Dodge City, Ford and Bucklin Railroad hauls tourists in the summer and grain and other freight during the off-season. For folks who pay the $10 adult fare to ride eight miles to the Willroads grain elevator and eight miles back, it is an hour and a half of pure history.

"This is a fun thing, you know," Dick Ranney said. "If you don't enjoy it, you shouldn't even be in it, because it's an awful lot of hard work."

Once you climb aboard the dining car, lounge car or combined baggage and passenger car, you step back in time. As the train jerks and starts, guitarist Carl Clare and fiddle player Paul Schneider tune up their instruments in the passenger car, while big-band music plays over loudspeakers in the World War II-era lounge car.

"What we usually do, when people get on here and the train is up to full speed — about 12 miles an hour — we start playing," Clare said. "Because see, they can't get off. We've got 'em trapped."

Climb to the back of the passenger car, and you'll see the same type of rest room that passengers saw in 1919, when the car was built. Peg Ranney said the toilet has been the hit of many school field trips.

"The stool goes up, and you can see the rails go whizzing by, just like the old days," she said. "Kids are always real amazed to see that." (But never fear, she noted. There's a modern flush toilet in the lounge car.)

Passengers are able to get out and stretch their legs when the trip is halfway through, while the crew turns the train around and readies it for the journey back. In the meantime, the Ranneys give each passenger a penny, which the train flattens into a nice little souvenir.

That exercise is also a safety lesson, Peg said. "It shows them how heavy these units really are. I tell the kids, 'This is why you should tell your mom and dad never to try and beat a train across a track.' They see how big these cars are — about 100 tons each — and they understand why it can't stop as fast as a car, even if it's only going 15 miles an hour."

The railroad is a work in progress. The Ranneys worked with the town of Ford to renovate its depot and turn it into a gift shop and crafts store. Renovations to another depot in nearby Bucklin are almost complete. In addition, they are renovating an old steam engine that they bought and had shipped from an old line in South Dakota.

"Everything has been kind of slow, because it's hard to find the funding to finish," Peg Ranney said. "We were a little naive when we started, I guess, but we've enjoyed it."

Large groups receive special rates on their 16-mile trip down the Dodge City, Ford and Bucklin line, but don't ask about senior citizen discounts. The senior citizens who struggle to keep this train going would just laugh.

"This is a much younger person's job," Peg Ranney said. "But somehow, we manage."

It's been worth it, she said. Whenever they get discouraged, they remember that they are keeping part of the Old West alive for future generations to enjoy.

"Once they take those rails out, then the railroad is gone forever," Peg said. "We just couldn't sit and watch that happen. But everyone — and us included — thought we had to be out of our minds.

"But we were just really interested in seeing that Kansas not lose any more modes of transportation. The big lines, they don't really care about small towns like these. They just want to put 90 to 150 cars on at once and go straight from coast to coast without stopping. But these small lines are part of our history."

Father of the Festival

Annual gathering in Winfield is sweet music to Bob Redford

Winfield

Every September in Winfield, music fills the air.

People from around the country meet there, where the Walnut River snakes through the prairie in south-central Kansas. They come to play, or just to listen. Some stay overnight in tents or camper trailers, building campfires, sharing stories, meeting old friends. But most of all, they come for the music — the sound of guitars, banjos, fiddles, mandolins and thousands of voices drifting through the valley like butterflies.

It's called the Walnut Valley Festival, and it happens because of a man named Bob Redford.

"It's like getting 10,000 people together that are all family," Redford said. "It's a big family reunion."

The reunion started in 1972, when Redford, an insurance agent and active member of the local Jaycees, and his wife, Kendra, decided that an autumn music festival would be a good way to

Redford says he doesn't play a note of anything.

seemed like a good way to do it."

Since the first festival, which was fraught with bad weather —"we had frost on our sleeping bags," Redford said — the annual attendance has grown to more than 12,000 people. The 1993 festival drew visitors from every state and at least 17 foreign countries.

"We have a lot of room, capacity for everyone to come, camp out and enjoy it for a couple of days," Redford said. "Forget about the outside world."

That's easy to do during the festival, when the only thing you have to worry about is getting to the right stage in time to see your favorite band. The atmosphere, like the acoustic music, is laid-back and barefoot, an island of serenity about 20 miles south of Wichita.

But it's not easy putting this show together. Redford supervises everything, from the bands to the concession stands to the National Flat-Picking Championship, which takes place every year during the festival.

Redford started the festival primarily to increase people's exposure to acoustic music in all forms. At this festival, you can hear Irish folk music and American country and western, rock and gospel, jazz and blues and everything in between.

At this festival, nationally renowned folk singers play alongside amateurs. And Redford, who considers himself anything but musically inclined, likes it that way.

"I don't play a note of anything, and I have

to work very hard to play a good radio," he said.

But that doesn't mean Redford, like thousands of other spectators, can't appreciate good music. When a professional fiddle player teams up with an amateur guitarist and first-time banjo plucker around the campfire one night, all the better.

"They're here because it's competition, it's entertainment, it's workshops and learning," he said. "It's a chance to do something a little different."

Some folks have been coming to Winfield since the first year of the festival. Others have only been once. Some will finally make it down for the first time this year. Regardless, everyone seems to know Redford, the man who put the bluegrass in Winfield.

"I get 500 to 600 hugs every year," he said. "That makes it all worth doing."

bring people to Winfield. The city used to host an annual motorcycle race at the local fairgrounds, but the ever-growing group of bikers got to be too much for the community.

"We were looking for something that would be well-accepted, where a lot of people could come together in a peaceful way," Redford said. "This

Bob Redford coordinates setup for the annual Walnut Valley Festival at the fairgrounds in Winfield.

Music Lover

Through his position at Friends University, Cecil Riney shares his passion

Wichita

The Friends University Singing Quakers are a Wichita musical institution. And so is Cecil Riney, the man with his back to the audience, punching the air and waving frantically.

Riney has directed the Singing Quakers, a well-known university choir, since 1960. That is the year he accepted a position as chairman of the fine arts division and coordinator of graduate studies at Friends University.

Riney was a member of the Singing Quakers when he was working toward his bachelor of music degree at Friends. Years later, after Riney had earned his doctor of musical arts degree from the University of Southern California, the former Quakers director resigned to take a position in Oklahoma City. Shortly thereafter the president of Friends asked Riney if he would like to return to Wichita to take over the reputable choir.

"I was very pleased to have the opportunity to come back," Riney said.

Except for a time in high school when he considered becoming a basketball coach, Riney always knew he wanted music to be a big part of his life. For one thing, a love of music ran in his family.

"Both my parents were musicians. My father was a church choir director, and my mother played the piano and organ," he said. "I played the trumpet in the band and sang in choirs. Music has always been a pretty dominant part of my life."

As director of the Singing Quakers, Riney likes sharing his passion with young people.

"I suppose the most gratifying thing about my job is working with college students," he said. "Seeing them develop musically, socially, academically and spiritually is a true joy."

In addition to teaching classes, directing the choir, producing major musical programs such as the Christmas Candlelight Concert, and touring each spring with the Singing Quakers, Riney often serves as guest conductor for festival and community choruses. He served as director of the Wichita Symphony Chorus during the 1993-94 concert season, as part of the symphony's 50th anniversary.

Cecil Riney conducts a rehearsal with the Friends University Singing Quakers.

He was selected as Kansas Musician of the Year in 1973 by Kansas Musical Clubs, and in 1993 he received the Governor's Arts Award from the Kansas Arts Commission.

At work in the choral room at Friends, he demands perfection, stopping during numbers to clean up sloppy entrances, strengthen weak vowels or inspire dispassionate voices.

"Music is the great communicating art, a universal art that touches almost everyone to some degree," he said.

He and his students learned that firsthand in the summer of 1994 when they performed in concert halls, churches and cathedrals throughout eastern Europe. "It was a real challenge, but it was wonderful," he said.

Riney's wife, Verna, and their two children are continuing the family tradition of music. Verna Riney has a music degree and teaches piano. Their son, Douglas, is music director at Hutchinson High School, and their daughter, Michelle, also teaches music in area schools. Both children have masters in music degrees from Friends.

Riney said he hopes his teaching inspires students and instills in them a lifelong love of music.

"If a student says that participation in the group during his college career helped change his life or enrich his life, I suppose that would be the highest compliment."

SNAPSHOT BIOGRAPHY

Cecil Riney was born Nov. 4, 1931, in Liberal. He later moved with his family to Stafford, where he graduated from high school. He has a bachelor of music degree from Friends University, a master of music from the University of Kansas and a doctor of musical arts from the University of Southern California. He and his wife, Verna, were married Aug. 10, 1951, in Stafford. He moved to Wichita in 1960 to become chairman of the fine arts division and coordinator of graduate studies in music at Friends University, a position he still holds today. Years in Kansas: 59.

Cecil Riney is chairman of the fine arts division at Friends and director of the Singing Quakers.

105

Outspoken and Opinionated

For cap maker Jerry Rutherford, speaking his mind is a way of life

Bucyrus

Jerry Rutherford had had enough of big-city attitudes, big-city traffic and those annoying big-city salesmen.

"By the time you got through answering the phone for every derelict wanting to sell you something over the phone, every salesman who comes knocking on your door, selling everything from light bulbs to toilet paper that never wears out, you just got tired of having your time filled chasing off people trying to make a buck hustling on the street. I got aggravated with it," he said.

"To do business with me, you've definitely got to come here."

This is Bucyrus, a bedroom community just south of Kansas City. And this is Jerry Rutherford. He owns a company that makes ball caps and decorates T-shirts, and he has some definite opinions about the American government and guys like him.

"The U.S. government is the small businessman's biggest enemy. Totally biggest enemy," he said. "Where can a small businessman get together with 750 of his cohorts and vote himself a $23,000 pay raise? And have someone who has no say-so in it, pay it?"

Watch out, Rush Limbaugh. Rutherford is on a roll.

"Very little clothing is put together in this country. So it's not a matter of fighting the imports. It's finding that niche to where you can survive along with them," he said. "Where you can survive with the government, you can survive with the imports, you can survive with the powers that be. It's a survival game."

Rutherford and a partner own The Shirt Hole and Krazzee Kappe Co., one of the smallest American cap makers. Foreign competitors have most of the business, and that irks him.

"We've had the meat taken away from us, and now we get the bones," he said. "But the bones are better than zero."

The caps are actually made at a factory in Kansas City. But at his home and workshop in Bucyrus, Rutherford has the freedom to run his company — and speak his mind.

Words pour quickly out of Rutherford's mouth, as if he has a subliminal alarm clock that will buzz at any second, signaling that his time is up.

"The imports, the offshore money, is coming in and gobbling us up. And me, as a small businessman, I can't stop it," he says. "I might as well jump in front of that train on the tracks out there and go, 'Whoa!' at 80 miles an hour. And the last thing I'm going to see is my head splattered all over the front of it.

"That's just like trying to fight the government or the imports. You don't. You try to figure out a way not to get in front of that train, not to get on that train, but to survive around that train."

To survive, Rutherford's company deals in small orders, quantities too small for foreign manufacturers to touch. He survives by making Krazzee Kappe caps for organizations and businesses that "still believe in American products and the American work ethic" and either can't or don't want to buy 60,000 caps at once.

"I like the idea that somebody puts enough faith in me to do something for them. I can perform the stunt, get it done, get it to them when they want it, how they want it, and they pay me. There's great satisfaction in that."

There is also great satisfaction in being outspoken and opinionated. For Rutherford, it's a way of business and a way of life.

"I open my mouth and just spew my guts out, and that way they don't sour. . . . I'm just like a low-rent politician," he said. "But at least I admit it."

Jerry Rutherford puts the final touches on a personalized ball cap in his shop in Bucyrus, just south of Kansas City.

NO PUBLIC RESTROOM
NO PUBLIC PHONE
NOT AN IMFORMATION BOOTH
STRICTLY GARMENTS & GARMENT DECORATION

GO AWAY

Jerry Rutherford was born June 27, 1946, in Des Moines, Iowa. He attended the University of Kansas, where he earned his bachelor's degree in fine arts. He and his wife, Diana, were married in August 1971, in Raytown, Mo. They have two children. Years in Kansas: 31.

Jerry Rutherford says he's just like a low-rent politician. "But at least I admit it," he says.

Bluebird Fan

Glenn Schmitt builds houses to help out his feathered friends

Halstead

Want to see a bluebird? We're talking about real bluebirds, genuine Kansas bluebirds, not sparrows or wrens or barn swallows. And for goodness' sake, we're not talking about blue jays. Those are birds, and they're blue, but they're not bluebirds.

Hang around with Glenn Schmitt long enough on a spring afternoon, and you just might see a real bluebird.

Schmitt is the biggest, most loyal fan of bluebirds in all of Harvey County, and probably the entire state. For four years — ever since he retired and closed his body shop in downtown Halstead — he has been building bluebird houses, attaching them to fence posts and watching what happens.

SNAPSHOT BIOGRAPHY

Glenn Schmitt was born Feb. 14, 1918, in Halstead. He graduated from high school and then served in the U.S. Army Air Corps for four years during World War II. He and his wife, Julia, were married Aug. 3, 1943. They have two children. Years in Kansas: 75.

He figures he's made close to 500 houses so far.

"The bluebird, I guess I just think he needs more help then the rest of 'em," Schmitt said.

Indeed, they do. Bluebirds used to be abundant in Kansas, but because of pesticides, a lack of natural nesting holes and increasing competition from other species, they are now rare. Schmitt, a naturalist by heart, wants to keep the little fellas around.

"If people could only see them, they'd see why I do this," he said. "That little male, when the sun hits directly on his back, well, you've just never seen

anything so blue. It's the prettiest color you've ever seen."

The bluebird houses are simple, rectangular boxes made from whatever wood Schmitt can find. He cuts a tiny oval into the front side — one and three-eighths inches wide by two inches tall — and attaches one of the sides with hinges, so he can check the boxes during the season and clean them out after the birds fly south. He either puts the houses out himself, usually hooking them to fence posts in Harvey County Park, or gives them to friends and friends-of-friends to attract bluebirds where they live.

He got the idea after reading a story in a wildlife magazine about a Montana man who, in his quest to save the mountain bluebird, built more than 18,000 birdhouses. "I thought that if these people out in Montana can account for 18,000 boxes, well, I used to take cars apart and put them back together, so I figured I could make some bird boxes."

He puts the boxes out in February, and beginning about mid-April, Schmitt climbs into his old Dodge, grabs his binoculars and goes searching.

"I had two families use that one last year," he says as he drives past one of the boxes in Harvey County Park. "I checked it this year, and nothing."

Still driving, still searching. Bluebirds are skittish birds, and they can be hard to spot. As he drives, he points out boxes and gives brief progress reports: "Nothing in that one . . . Five eggs there . . . Nest in that one, but it's a sparrow . . . Nothing there . . ."

Last spring, Schmitt and a friend sat several feet from a box and watched a pair of bluebirds building their nest. It was the first time his friend had ever seen a bluebird, so they watched for almost two hours. Even for Schmitt, it was quite a show.

"Boy, they sure were busy," he said. "They looked like they'd been goofing off, and they just realized they needed to get this nest-building project under way. And that male, I really think he was showing off."

Today's search, however, is not so lucky. Not a bluebird in sight. But just as Schmitt gives up for the day and heads back toward home, his eye catches a flash of blue on a nearby fence. He screeches the Dodge to a halt so quickly that the binoculars go rolling along the floorboard.

There he is! Perched precariously on a fence wire about 10 feet from one of Schmitt's boxes is a male bluebird, his back feathers so blue they look almost violet. The color is in sharp contrast to his front feathers, which are a deep chestnut red.

"That's why I say he's got the sky on his back and the sun on his chest," Schmitt said. "Isn't that the prettiest blue you've ever seen? You just can't duplicate it."

After several minutes, the bird twitches, nods and flutters away. Schmitt marks the day a success and starts the car.

"I think God put every living creature on this earth for a purpose, and it's up to us to figure out what it is," he said. "I think the bluebird's purpose is to show us how beautiful nature can be."

Glenn Schmitt checks on one of his bluebird houses near Harvey County Park. For four years he has been building the houses.

Pearl Shivers always has plenty of pie on hand.

SNAPSHOT BIOGRAPHY

Pearl Shivers was born Oct. 5, 1904, in Alton, Mo. She and her husband, the late Samuel Shivers, were married Sept. 5, 1940, in Denton, Texas. They had two sons, Bill and Robert. Years in Kansas: 51.

Chez Pearl

Pearl Shivers is still enjoying people, making pies at age 89

Eureka

That's an 89-year-old woman back there in the kitchen, cooking up enough beef brisket, chicken-fried steak, mashed potatoes, peas, beans, rolls and pie to feed the dozens of people who will visit the City Cafe for Sunday lunch.

Her name is Pearl Shivers, but you can call her Pearl.

"I should get rid of this cafe, because I'm too old to be running it," she said, smiling.

That's not likely. Because after all the work Shivers puts in at the cafe — and it's a lot of work, getting up at 2 a.m. and spending all morning in the kitchen — she enjoys the kind of rewards that only a small town like Eureka could provide.

"I like the people. I love the people," she said. She is a petite woman with snow-white hair, cat-eye glasses and a smile you can see from across the room. "I've been in the food business for a long time, and I really wouldn't want to do anything else."

Shivers grew up in a small town just east of Tulsa, Okla. In 1923, at age 19, she got her start in business by running a boardinghouse for employees of the Waite-Phillips Petroleum Co.

She moved to Eureka in 1940, shortly after she and her husband, Samuel Shivers, were married. He died in 1950, and Pearl continued her business career. She opened a "help-yourself laundry" in Eureka, then a restaurant, and later the City Cafe.

The cafe is the sort of place where food is served in heaping spoonfuls, walls are decorated with pictures of John Wayne, and the folks at the next table are just like family. A carved-wood sign over the kitchen door says "Pearl's Kitchen" in simple print letters. And when the noted chef needs a break after preparing for the lunchtime crowd, she goes upstairs for a little nap.

That's the way life is in a small town, Shivers said, and she likes it. People in Eureka care about one another.

"If they have trouble, you have trouble. If I have trouble, they have trouble," she said. "You get involved in each other's lives."

But when you're eating with Pearl, there's no trouble. What there is is a big ol' piece of pie with your name on it.

"I think what we sell more of than anything else is coconut pie," she said.

And who wouldn't love this pie, smooth and creamy, with just the right amount of flaky coconut? Don't like coconut, you say? Not to worry. There's plenty of apple, cherry, strawberry rhubarb, lemon and chocolate cream.

"You like that, do you?" Shivers said, her eyes gleaming. She is out of the kitchen now and tending the cash register, talking with customers on their way out the door. Her smile is as bright and her math as accurate as it ever was, despite newfangled, unpredictable technology.

"Our old machine's getting serviced, and this one's a loaner," she said, punching each button deliberately. "Oh, well, here's your change, anyway."

Everyone loves Pearl, from the busy waitresses to the toddler over there begging for another bite of pie. And Pearl loves this place.

"I enjoy people," she said. "I'd get awfully lonesome in a rocking chair."

Pearl Shivers, center, is "Mom" to her long-term employees.

Collecting History

Forrest Shmidl has been picking up pieces of the past for most of his life

Medicine Lodge

Music from an old-time record player sets the mood for a visit to Forrest Shmidl's personal museum in Medicine Lodge.

He's been collecting pieces of American history for most of his life.

"I would love to be able to spend an hour with the people who invented these things," he said.

Spend an hour with Shmidl, and you'll learn a lot about pioneer ingenuity.

"This is a buffalo skinner," he said, pulling a metal contraption off one wall of his cluttered shed. It looked like a cross between a tooth-edged wrench and a tow rope.

"The old-timers, all they was wanting was the hide, so they'd skin the legs up, and they would clamp these on," he said. "These teeth weren't sharp enough that they'd hurt the hide.

"Clamp that on, and then hook the horse to this, and pull the hide off the buffalo.

"I've just always been interested in old things. It started with some things that I just couldn't bear to get rid of," he said. "I guess I'm what you might call a pack rat."

He gathers his treasures by visiting flea markets, estate sales, auctions and antique stores throughout Kansas and everywhere he travels. He doesn't sell anything, but he is open to trades every now and then.

"I don't like to have two of anything. One is all I want. If I ever have an extra, that's for trading."

For Shmidl, who has spent years collecting and researching these artifacts, each piece is a treasure.

"This is what they screwed into the horseshoes in the wintertime, when the horses had to walk on ice," he said, holding a metal spike about the size of a big bullet. "There was four of these in each shoe."

Shmidl has collected all sorts of weird and wonderful things. And he likes nothing better than to hold up some strange contraption and ask a visitor to guess what it is.

"What do you think?"

Hmmm. A soup ladle? A miniature snow shovel?

"Actually, what it is, it's a hearing aid," he said. "Put it in this way."

He held the tip of the long metal handle to his ear, so it looked like the big ladle was growing out of his head. The "cup" end of the gizmo collects sound and sends it into the earpiece. Amazing.

Shmidl also has a collection of more than 500 decorative or antique doorknobs. A gold-colored one has "Public Schools, City of New York" engraved into it. Another, shaped like a Coca-Cola bottle, was the handle to the screen door from an old store.

He also owns hundreds of old keys — the kind with the fancy, ornate decorations, not the modern ones made at discount stores.

"I call this my memory board," he said, "because this is the keys to all my old girlfriends' houses."

Several years ago, one of Shmidl's pieces — a Japanese flag found on the battlefield of Okinawa in 1945 — was flown to Japan by one of Shmidl's neighbors and returned to its rightful owners.

He discovered the importance of the flag by accident, when he asked the neighbor, a native of Japan, to interpret the writing on the flag.

She told him that during the war, it was Japanese custom to have friends and relatives sign a soldier's flag before he went to battle. Each signature meant a prayer and messages of good luck. Using the inscriptions as clues, the woman tracked down the soldier's family and returned the flag during a trip to Japan.

Shmidl said the experience convinced him how important it is to preserve and protect pieces of history.

"I don't know anything that I could have done that would have made me any happier," he said.

Among Shmidl's odd collection of antiques, artifacts, keys and doorknobs is something more — an appreciation for life's other treasures.

"So what else can you ask for? You have your food, clothing, beautiful neighbors, wonderful town, wonderful wife and family and dear friends," he said.

"What else from life do you want?"

Lyndall and Forrest Shmidl look over items in the museum behind their home in Medicine Lodge.

Karen Day Smith and her husband, Terry, enjoy a game of Scrabble.

Getting It Done

Look past the disability, Karen Day Smith asks, and you'll see the person

McPherson

If you want to feel good about life, talk to Karen Day Smith.

"There are days when I do get depressed, but it doesn't last very long."

When she was 5, Smith was diagnosed with spinal muscular atrophy, a degenerative disease in the muscular dystrophy family of diseases. She started using a wheelchair in the eighth grade and now uses a motorized chair to get around her house in McPherson.

But even though her disability restricts her in some ways, she doesn't let it keep her down.

In 1977, she left her little town of Burrton to go to college at Emporia State University. There, she earned her associate degree in sociology. In 1981, she got a job as a clerk for First Federal Savings & Loan in Hutchinson.

"It was neat, because it was so hard for me to get a job," she said. "Not only because of my disability, but because there just weren't a lot of jobs out there."

Later that year, she appeared on the Jerry Lewis Labor Day Telethon to help raise money to fight muscular dystrophy. A few days after the telethon, she got a phone call from Terry Smith.

"He called me up, and we went out to lunch," she said. "After that, we just started dating. I was really apprehensive at first."

But her fears subsided, and in 1985 Terry and Karen were married.

"I forget she's in a wheelchair a lot of times," Terry Smith said.

"It's easy always being around Karen. She's always in a good mood and optimistic about everything, so I guess that rubs off on me a little bit."

A few years after their wedding, though, the disease that will eventually claim Karen Smith's life gave the couple a scare.

"I had been really tired, and I didn't know why I was so tired," Karen said. "So I went to the doctor, and he put me in the hospital, and I went into respiratory arrest."

She now uses a ventilator at night to keep her lungs moving, and she had to quit her job and stay home. Even so, Karen keeps busy with new and exciting challenges.

Now, she does cross-stitch and paints decorative wood crafts.

"I've always enjoyed doing painting, but never had the time," she said. "And now that I have the time to do it, I thought, why not?

"I picked up on it really fast . . . and I really enjoy it."

As she paints, her dog, Peanut, a terrier-dachshund mix, is always nearby. He stays nested close by the wheels of her chair.

"He's with me every minute, everywhere I go, if he can be," she said. "He's a good little guy."

At the Smith home in McPherson, there's a wheelchair, a respirator and a terrible disease. But that doesn't bother the loving people who live there.

"My family doesn't think of me as being handicapped, just as a normal person, and I think that's really helped," Karen said.

"I really don't do that much for her. She does everything for herself," her husband said. "I don't have to do special things for her or anything. She just does it. It may take her a little longer, but she gets the job done."

Gets it done, and never forgets to enjoy life.

"We have limited time, and we cherish every moment," she said.

"Make the most of every minute," he added.

And if Karen Smith had a message to leave with people, it is this: "If you look past the disability, you can see the person."

SNAPSHOT BIOGRAPHY

Karen Day Smith was born Aug. 5, 1959, in Long Beach, Calif. She moved to Burrton when she was 2 years old and graduated from Burrton High School in 1977. She received her associate degree in sociology from Emporia State University in 1981. She and her husband, Terry, were married March 23, 1985, in Burrton. Years in Kansas: 33.

Karen Day Smith's dog, Peanut, is always near as she works on craft projects.

Always Looking Up
Randy Smith has carved an opportunity out of adversity

Turon

Some people complain about the unfairness of life. Some, when faced with illness and adversity, give up.

Others, like Randy Smith, pick up the pieces and make something useful.

"I wake up in the morning, and I'm thankful to be alive. I'm thankful to wake up in the morning," Smith said. "I'm thankful to get out of bed."

Smith is a woodworker. He likes to say he "recycles trees." Out of scrap pieces of wood that people give him, he fashions toys, tables or anything else people might buy. It is a source of income, albeit modest, but more than that, it keeps Smith going.

An insulin-dependent diabetic since he was 5, Smith has an eye disorder that has made him legally blind. He pushes his face right up close to the worktable while he carves, as if he were looking for tiny bugs in the wood. He also suffers from arthritis.

sign on the doorway of his wood shop that says, "Always look up." That kind of optimism helps Smith not only see the positive side of his own life, but also help others.

The walls of his shop are lined with letters from day-care centers throughout Stafford and Reno counties, thanking Smith for the toy cars, trucks and trains he has given them over the years. Smith calls the wheeled toys "putt-putts." He doesn't use drawings or patterns for any of his work.

"I can see like I'm looking through a telescope. I see about this far," he said, holding a hand about a foot from his face. Consequently, his shop is meticulously organized, with each tool in its proper place, right where he needs it. "If it's not where it's supposed to be, I can't see it."

Still, Smith saw an opportunity, developed a skill, and through imperfect eyes has found his future.

"I am given strength by God," he said. "I love life. I love being alive. I like taking an opportunity and seeing what I can do with it."

Smith started working with wood as a youngster, when he would hang around at construction sites in Turon until someone gave him a job. In high school, a shop teacher taught him how to draw up his own plans and craft things out of wood.

His first project — a lamp made out of a piece of driftwood that an uncle gave to his mother — is still in his house.

He finds that the wood — uneven, complete with

Smith with his multi-wood combine and train.

wormholes and other imperfections — is a lot like life. No one's perfect, but we all keep trying.

"We're barely making it. I'm on disability. My wife is down at the restaurant washing dishes," he said. "I'm doing this because I enjoy it, and I'm also able to make a little money off of it, but we're just getting by.

"But I'm thankful to have what I got. . . . It's not 'til you lose something that you realize what you lost."

Smith hopes others will see his work and adopt his philosophy.

"I want people to realize that no matter how tough the situation, just pick up the pieces. Make the most of what you have."

But as long as he's working with wood, he's happy.

"Wood is a gift from God. It's one of those things you don't take for granted," he said. "I'm on disability, I've got health problems from head to toe, but I don't take anything for granted."

Smith could have given up. Instead, he hung a

Opposite: Randy Smith is happy as long as he's working on wood, such as on this table at his home in Turon. He uses forks from trees as table legs.

Gentleman Retiree

Omie Spohn has given up his farm but not his garden

Fredonia

They once called him the gentleman farmer.

Folks around Fredonia, and even as far away as Neodesha, Independence and Wichita, used to watch for the classified ad that Omie Spohn would put in the local paper whenever his tomatoes were ready to harvest. They'd come and buy whatever he had, and visit another time for beans, peas and cantaloupe.

He doesn't have the farm anymore. About two

Omie Spohn mulches his tomatoes early in the garden season. He gives them away.

years ago, he and his wife, Irma, thought it was time they started retiring for real, and they moved to a house in town.

But Omie still has a little garden, a 30-by-30-foot collection of peas, cabbage, okra and parsnips. And every now and then he'll get a call on the telephone: "When are your tomatoes gonna be ready?"

"I'm through selling at market, so now I just give 'em away," Spohn said. "Whatever my wife and I can't use, we give to the friends and neighbors."

Farming was not always a way of life for Spohn. For 18 years, he owned and operated a local car dealership. After retiring from that, he bought a 46-acre farm about one and a half miles northwest of town.

He and his wife cleaned it up, reconstructed the pond that was on site, built a modular home and bought a herd of Hereford cattle. He did it because he loved the lifestyle.

"It's a lot of work," he said of his gardening. "But that is the way I enjoy my retirement."

He spent hours planting, watering and tending marigolds and other flowers, not for himself, but because they made other people happy.

"I get good out of it, too, because it makes them happy, and I'm happy," said Spohn, a soft-spoken, bespectacled man. "As you can see, I never get done with all my work here, and for me, that is retirement.

"These plants, they talk to me. They keep me awake. And so for me, this is retirement, but still working every day, seeing these cabbages grow, tomatoes grow. Just everything in general appeals to me. There's just nothing about it I don't like."

In his garden, Spohn is at peace.

"When I was in business, that mental strain was

harder on me than this physical work."

On the old Spohn farm, work was calling the cattle — "Come on, people! Come on, you people!" — and feeding them right out of his bucket.

"They're just like humans to me. Oh, yes, I love them, and you see they're tame. See, a lot of cattle, a stranger come out like this and they'll run. These here, they're pets."

And if you thought people came from miles around just to buy a head of Spohn's famous cabbage or see the steers, think again. They also loved Spohn's other pets — his pond full of 12- to 15-pound channel catfish.

"Come on, you fish! Come on, you fish, come on!" Spohn would call as he scattered a bucket of food pellets on the pond water. Dozens of catfish would flop along the surface, their eyes and whiskers peeking out above the water.

"I have a nephew in Wichita, and one time, he and a friend drove to southeast Kansas to see Big Brutus. You know about Big Brutus?" Spohn said, referring to the giant coal-mining machine on display in the town of West Mineral.

"On their way back, they decided they'd stop and see Uncle Omie's catfish. So they came by, and we went out to feed 'em. And my nephew's friend said, 'This is better than Big Brutus.'"

These days, the Mennonite farmer who bought Spohn's old farm makes sure the catfish stay fed. And Spohn, he makes sure his little crop of peas and parsnips is doing all right. It's a gentlemanly kind of retirement, and he likes it just fine.

"I guess to a lot of people, this wouldn't mean a whole lot," he said. "But to me, it's heaven right here on earth."

SNAPSHOT BIOGRAPHY

Omie Spohn was born Jan. 24, 1912, in Fredonia. He graduated from Fredonia High School in 1933 and attended Fredonia Business College. He and his wife, Irma, were married June 12, 1935. They have three daughters. Years in Kansas: 82.

Omie Spohn in his garden.

"These plants, they talk to me. They keep me awake. And so for me, this is retirement, but still working every day, seeing these cabbages grow, tomatoes grow. Just everything in general appeals to me. There's just nothing about it I don't like."

The Power of Love

Randy and Suzy Storms are "in there for the long haul"

Suzy and Randy Storms.

Wichita

The day Randy Storms, a quadriplegic, met Suzy Harsh, a divorced mother with two children, neither thought it would lead to love.

Suzy was hoping only for forgiveness. Her ex-husband, an alcoholic and gambling addict, had borrowed money from Storms several years earlier and had gambled it away. Although she had nothing to do with her ex-husband's habit, and despite the fact that her divorce was long over, Suzy felt guilty and wanted to set the record straight.

To Suzy, Randy was "that poor guy in the wheelchair." She didn't know what to say.

But that evening, they ended up talking for hours — first at Randy's house, and later over ice cream and bottomless cups of coffee at a local restaurant.

"At first, I kept thinking, 'Oh my God, what am I doing here? Am I a glutton for punishment, or what?'" Suzy said. "But it was like a quick bonding. We were on the same wavelength, and we ended up having a great time."

The rest, as a hopeless romantic might say, was history. But the Storms' courtship — and, later, their marriage — has not been easy.

Randy, a former athlete who played football, basketball and track at Wichita Collegiate High School, was paralyzed in a diving accident in 1981. He recovered from the accident but never recovered use of his legs or full use of his arms. He uses a wheelchair and requires help for everyday activities like shopping, bathing and even getting out of bed in the morning.

When he met Suzy, part of him wanted to keep a safe distance, not get too close, not get hurt. The other part just fell in love.

"I was putting her through this battery of tests,

opening up a little bit at a time," Randy said. "It was like, 'OK, now she knows this about me. Let's see if she likes me *now*.' And, 'OK, here's a little bit more. Let's see if she sticks around.'"

She stuck around. Of course, she had doubts of her own. Friends and family had discouraged her from developing a relationship with Randy, saying she didn't realize how difficult life with a quadriplegic could be. And once, one of her children even said, "You're not going to marry a guy in a wheelchair, are you?"

But Suzy kept meeting Randy for long talks or walks along the river, and love flourished.

"He is my soul mate, my best buddy. He's my lover, my sweetheart. He's my helper. He's everything in my life," she said. "I am better with him than without him."

"You know, I don't look good anymore by the world's standards. And I don't perform by the world's standards," Randy said. "And yet, when I look into her eyes, I don't have to."

On June 15, 1990, in an enormous wedding at Eastminster Presbyterian Church, Randy and Suzy were married.

Randy is volunteer director of Young Life, a Christian ministry program at high schools in Wichita, and he travels around the country sharing his story and speaking to young people about Jesus Christ. He also wrote a book, "Between the Lightning and the Thunder," that tells the story

of his accident and recovery.

He says his faith and Suzy's love have helped him deal with a tragedy some people would consider worse than death.

Recently, the Storms' son, Nick, was assigned to write a report about a person he admired, someone who had overcome a tragedy and was an inspiration to others. He wrote about Randy, and got an A-plus.

"Through Randy, I've learned that a person can deal with anything, survive it and be strengthened by it," Suzy said.

"It's all an attitude," he said. "When we took our vows, we took each other for better or worse, and there's been both. But we're in there for the long haul. And by God's grace, we're gonna make it."

Suzy and Randy Storms ended up talking for hours the first day they met. "We were on the same wavelength," Suzy says.

Lawrence "Bud" Strawder has taken his "baby pig" — a realistic hand puppet — to New York and London.

Country Critter

You won't see puppet maker Lawrence Strawder wearing a fancy suit

Burlington

Lawrence "Bud" Strawder has traveled to New York City at least once a year for the past 15 years, and he's figured out how to keep the muggers away.

He carries a skunk.

Not a real skunk, mind you, but one of the plush, realistic-looking hand puppets made by Country Critters Inc., Strawder's company in Burlington.

"I just take my little skunk and walk down Broadway going like this," Strawder said, using one hand to bring the toy's body to life and the other to bounce its tail up and down.

"Everybody gets off the sidewalk. You don't even have to watch where you're going. . . . I've never had a bit of trouble."

Never a bit of trouble. That's the way Strawder likes to live and work. The philosophy has made Country Critters one of the largest puppet manufac-

strate them at fairs and festivals. The puppets sold well, but the Strawders felt that if they could look more realistic, be better made, be easier to operate and, above all, be made in the United States, they would sell even better.

In 1980, with three employees, Country Critters began. The puppets were a hit from the start, and in 1986 the company started making plush toys. Lawrence Strawder bought out his brother's interest in the business in 1987, and he continues to own and operate the company today.

"I had no idea it would develop this much," he said.

But it did. And part of the company's success is Strawder's image. For instance, you'll never see this businessman in an Armani suit.

"I'd really rather go to jail than put on a tie. . . . I'm a farmer, I'm proud of it, and I really don't care what people think."

People see him as a down-home, aw-gee kind of guy. And the image is real.

"When I go to the trade show in New York, I'll be

animal, but we try to give them a personality," he said. Sure enough, the bandit-faced raccoon sprang to life.

"Now that you really know how to operate him, you wonder what that little dickens would do," he said, using one hand to animate the raccoon and the other to cradle the animal in his arms. "He'd probably crawl up there and get that pencil out of my pocket."

No sooner did Strawder say the words, than the frisky animal pulled the pencil out of those bib overalls, held it in his paws and started to sniff the eraser. Wait a second . . . maybe that is a real raccoon. It looks so alive, so cute, so smart.

"They're real smart," Strawder said, grinning. "They learn real fast."

So does Strawder, an old-fashioned businessman who uses corn grinders and grain bin dryers in the making of his puppets.

And he hasn't forgotten the most important corporate philosophy: Have a little fun. Whether he's raising eyebrows on the streets of New York or playing with his gigantic toy gorilla at the factory — "Sometimes people say, 'Which one is the monkey?' " — this company president would rather sit on his Papa Bear stuffed animal than sit on a board of directors.

"I feel at home."

SNAPSHOT BIOGRAPHY

Lawrence Strawder was born Aug. 2, 1930, in rural Le Roy. He attended a country school for grades one through eight and graduated from Burlington High School in 1947. He and his wife, Velma, were married June 9, 1949, in Le Roy. They have four children. Years in Kansas: 64.

---

turers in the world, selling its products in more than 5,000 stores in the United States and shipping to 17 foreign countries.

Strawder's first foray into the puppet business was in 1977, when S&S Sales, a company he and his brother Jim owned, acquired hand puppets that had been made in Korea. To sell the puppets, the company sent 13 crews all over the country to demon-

wearing my old bib overalls just like this.

"When I get off the plane in New York, people look at me kinda funny, and they say, 'You must be from Kansas.' I don't know how they figure that out."

Country Critters puppets look like regular toys on the factory floor. But put one of those raccoon puppets on Strawder's hand, and watch it come to life.

"We not only try to make them look like a real

123

Joy in the Country

Ann Thornburg and her husband have left behind big-city stress

Yoder

Come and sit, Ann Thornburg said. Come and sit on the wooden porch swing, and watch those crazy people driving to the city.

"They're like little ants," she said. "I come out in the morning with my coffee, and I swing on this swing, and I sit here and think, 'You poor fools. Don't you know how much neater it is when you sit here and watch the people driving by and going to work?' "

Thornburg knows what that was like. She and her husband, Dale, used to live in Wichita, working for high-tech computer and aircraft industries. But then fate — a strange combination of job layoffs, stress and an intriguing opportunity to manage a country gift shop — changed the Thornburgs' outlook on life.

Here's how it happened: In 1985, Dale was laid off from his job at Learjet. The computer company Ann worked for wanted to put a terminal in her house. She had always been on call 24 hours a day for emergencies, but the home computer, which would hook up to her phone line, would make her even more accessible to the company.

"I came home from work that day, and I said, 'Dale, I can't do this anymore.' And he said, 'Well, then quit.' And it was so amazing, because until that moment, I really hadn't thought about that as an option. But then I said, 'Yeah, why not?' "

She did quit, and the couple moved to Yoder, an Amish and Mennonite farming community in Reno County. The barn behind their house had previously been converted into And Cousins Make Three, a gift shop owned by Ann and two cousins, so the Thornburgs took over the shop.

Looking back, they miss things like regular paychecks and paid vacation. But they don't miss much else.

"You don't have to live like that," Ann Thornburg said. "I don't care what kind of cocoon they think they have you in. You don't have to. You can live on less. You can do with less. You don't have to put up with it, so I don't."

Her husband agreed. "At first, when you're used to a paycheck every two weeks, you know how much money you have coming. Yes, it is quite a difference," he said. "You think a lot about, 'Am I going to have enough?' But we've made it so far."

The 18,000-square-foot shop, originally a seed-cleaning barn, is packed from floor to ceiling with handmade clothes, dolls, artwork and other items, most of them made by about 150 Kansas artists. The outside is painted with bright red, yellow and blue flowers, making it easy to spot from the road. In a nearby garage, Dale crafts handmade cradles and other wood treasures to sell in the shop.

"This is real relaxing for me. I don't watch that much TV, so this is the way I spend my time," he said. "It keeps me out of the local pool hall in Yoder. But of course, they don't have one."

The Thornburgs share an adjoining pasture with an Amish farm family, and they keep a dog, a few cats and several peacocks in their back yard. This year, a barn swallow built a nest just inside the barn door out back, and Ann likes to show visitors how the seven chicks poke their heads over the top edge of the nest.

"Isn't that cute?" she said. "One of the little joys of the country."

There are lots of little joys, and they add up to a way of life that Ann and Dale Thornburg wouldn't trade for a return ticket to the city.

"It's so nice and quiet out here," Dale said. "I suppose that while your kids are growing up, there are a few more advantages to staying in a bigger city.

"But when they're grown up, it's to your advantage to get out of town fast."

Ann Thornburg sells craft items in her shop, And Cousins Make Three.

Dale and Ann Thornburg's shop near Yoder offers handmade clothes, dolls, artwork and other items. Dale makes the wooden chairs.

A Quiet Road

Tracy and Margaret Turnbull are happy at home in Belvidere

Belvidere

Margaret Turnbull is the last native of Belvidere who stuck around.

She and her husband, Tracy, own and operate the Trail's End Junke Shop, an end-of-the-paved-road, friendly kind of place in a back-road, almost-forgotten kind of town.

Belvidere is in southeastern Kiowa County, on the northern cusp of the Gypsum Hills. It was founded in 1885 and once had a population of about 100. These days, Margaret and Tracy and their building full of antiques and secondhand goods are about all that's left. But that's all right with Margaret and Tracy.

"It's pretty peaceful," Margaret Turnbull said. "I haven't ever wanted to live anywhere else. He'll tell you that. I always got homesick wherever we traveled."

Life takes us down many roads. The road to the Turnbulls' place is a quiet one, but friendly. The sign in front of the Trail's End Junke Shop rocks back and forth, its squeak the only sound you hear over the breeze.

"There's always someone coming in," Margaret said. "Maybe no big buyers, but the fella after the cup of coffee is just as welcome as the one who is after the big piece of furniture."

"There's the feed truck now," Tracy said, pointing out the window. "He makes about three runs and then he stops for coffee."

For those of us who come from the cities, talking to the Turnbulls around the kitchen table is like being in Grandma's house.

"We just kinda made up our mind that we was going day by day," Margaret said. "I think what we've enjoyed about the people that have been here is just the visiting.

"Maybe of all the places we've been and all the things we've done, it just seems so comfortable. And to know your neighbor, and you can depend on him and trust him — it makes a lot of difference."

Years ago, six or eight trains a day were common through Belvidere. So were more businesses. So were more people. Now, Margaret Turnbull is the last resident of Belvidere to be born there.

"Oh, I know I'm special to somebody," she said, shrugging off the honor.

SNAPSHOT BIOGRAPHY

Tracy Turnbull was born Feb. 5, 1917, near Sullivan, Mo. He served in the U.S. Army during World War II. Margaret Cobb Turnbull was born Sept. 24, 1925, in Belvidere. She graduated from high school in Belvidere and attended American Business College in Wichita. They were married Dec. 20, 1960, in Webb City, Mo. Tracy Turnbull and his previous wife had three children, one of whom died in 1965. Years in Kansas: Tracy 30, Margaret 68.

People may wonder why Margaret and Tracy chose this little place over bigger, more exciting, more fast-paced cities. Places with scenic beaches or mountains, or skyscrapers that light up at night. For them, the answer is as simple as the water.

"There are a lot of people who come back," she said. "They always say, if you drink water from the Medicine River, you'll always come back."

And besides, Margaret said, Belvidere is fast-paced enough for them.

"People are always asking us what we do," she said. "And we run out of hours, we really do. It seems like our day is gone before we know it."

Another story, another cup of coffee, and the visit is gone before you know it, too. Not hard to see why Margaret and Tracy like it here, where time moves like sweet molasses, and the day's events will never be featured on the movie of the week.

"It's not that we're all that smart or anything. We just like it here, and that's why we're here," Tracy said.

"This is home," his wife added. "Mm-hmm, sure is."

Tracy and Margaret Turnbull share coffee and conversation with friends at their Trail's End Junke Shop.

Animal Lover

J.W. Vanderpool raises some exotic critters on his farm near Meade

Meade

The problem with ostrich meat, says J.W. Vanderpool, is all semantic.

"You don't say you're going to eat a cowburger, but that's what it is," he said. "If you said to some city folks, 'I think I'm going to eat the back leg off a hog today,' they wouldn't think too good of that. But you can have hamburger or beef or pork, and that seems to be all right. Well, it's the same with the ostriches. It's a problem with labeling."

So far, at least, folks seem to be skittish about eating huge birds with long eyelashes that bury their heads in the sand. Nevertheless, Vanderpool, who raises the fowl on his exotic-animal farm near Meade, says that someday the American carnivore will come around. In the meantime, he's trying to think of a good name for ostrich meat.

Vanderpool's place looks more like a zoo than a typical Kansas farm. Besides the dozens of ostriches — 25 adults and 30 youngsters, at last count — he has miniature Japanese deer, exotic decorative ducks, wallabies, rheas, emus, African pygmy hedgehogs, two komondor guard dogs from Hungary, a pair of reindeer and a pair of elk.

"As I get older, I keep getting crazier, and I love it," he said. "I'm still a farmer, always have been. Now I just farm some unusual critters."

It all started several years ago, when he trapped some bobcats and raised them as pets.

"We took 'em away from their mother when they were about nine days old, and we had to feed them every three hours, 24 hours a day. With an eyedropper at start, and then we moved over to a pet baby bottle," Vanderpool said. "And then after they got big enough, well, they'd come to the bottle, just like a regular pet of any other kind, you know."

But they weren't your average house cat, and Vanderpool eventually gave up raising bobcats in exchange for kinder, gentler creatures.

Like African pygmy hedgehogs. Vanderpool is convinced that these cute little rodents, needlelike quills and all, will be the next coveted house pet. He is so convinced, in fact, that he's got about 60 adult hedgehogs and dozens of babies in a little room on his exotic-animal ranch.

"I say your hedgehogs will be the best pet on the market today, barring the dog and cat — those animals that show affection to people," he said. "But of all those other kinds of animals — guinea pigs and rats and mice and potbellied pigs — I'd say the hedgehog has 'em all, hands down."

It takes a love of animals, a lot of patience and, most important, a sense of humor to run a ranch like this one, Vanderpool said. Those ostriches, for instance,

S N A P S H O T   B I O G R A P H Y

J.W. Vanderpool was born May 13, 1942, in Beaver, Okla. When he was 8, he moved with his family to a farm just outside Meade. He joined the U.S. Army in 1959 and served three years in Germany. He and his wife, Paulette, were married Oct. 19, 1963, in Purcell, Okla. They have one daughter. Years in Kansas: 44.

aren't the most intelligent birds in the world.

"I've known people who raised turkeys say that turkeys are the dumbest animals around. But apparently they've never raised ostriches," he said. The birds seem to exist in perpetual puberty, constantly running into things with their oversized, awkward legs. If an ostrich gets its head caught in something, such as a fence or gate, he'll pull until his head comes off.

And the other day, Vanderpool discovered that one of the birds had tried to eat a bone that was almost bigger than its head. The ostrich looked like a cartoon, with an oversized bone stuck in the middle of its long neck, so Vanderpool spent the morning sliding the bone back up the animal's throat.

"One thing about this business," he said. "You just never know what's gonna happen next."

Fortunately for Vanderpool, he's got about 1,800 acres of land and all the special papers and permits required to raise exotic animals. When groups of children visit his farm, he loves to see their eyes grow wide with excitement and surprise.

"I think people are starved to see these sorts of unusual, exotic animals. They think it's pretty neat, you know," he said. "And I do, too."

Vanderpool with two African pygmy hedgehogs.

J.W. Vanderpool says ostriches are far from being the most intelligent birds in the world. He raises them on his farm near Meade.

Billie Allen places a graduation cap on son Bobby Vaught's head. Vaught graduated from Cloud County Community College in May 1994.

Beating the Odds

Bobby Vaught is overcoming hurdles — on the track and otherwise

Wichita

Before Bobby Vaught became a nationally ranked hurdles champion at Cloud County Community College, he had to leap several hurdles of his own. And it took teamwork.

"As I looked around, I saw my friends getting arrested and going to jail, and I saw their lives going downhill, and that's not what I wanted to be. It frightened me," Vaught said.

But Vaught is a survivor. With the guidance and support of his mother, Billie Allen, and his former high school track coach, Steve Dodd, he has beaten the odds.

"His junior year, he was on the bubble. He could have gone either way," said Dodd, track coach at Wichita North High School. "And so many times, he'd come in, and I'd say, 'Bob, look at what you've got. You're not going to kiss all this off.'

"I didn't want to see this kid go down the toilet."

The statistics weren't in his favor. Vaught was a young black man without a lot of money, with a single mother struggling to keep her family going. He was prime gang material, and even he knew it.

"I came very close to that at one time, because it seemed like the more I tried to do right, the more I tried to better myself, there was always someone there to knock me down, to tell me, you know, 'Bob, you're never going to make it.'"

His mother remembers.

"Bobby got to high school, and there came a time when he wanted to sell drugs. I spent many a night laying in my bed awake," she said, "until I heard him come in, and I knew he was OK."

For this black teenager, it was his mother and his coach who made the difference, helped him clear the hurdle between failure and success. At one point, Dodd even gave the young athlete his running shoes.

"Growing up without a father, Coach kinda took over, took up where Dad kinda left off," Vaught said. "He spent so much time with me and helped me better myself that there came a point I couldn't let him down."

Dodd said it wasn't him, but rather Vaught's love of sports that helped him achieve success.

"I don't feel like I saved his life or anything. I feel like he saved himself," Dodd said. "I think track and sports in general did help this kid. Had we not had sports in our school, that kid would be lost. I think sports saved his life."

At Cloud County Community College, Vaught made good grades and continued to excel in track. In 1994, after being awarded a track scholarship to attend Wichita State University, he returned to Wichita to study. He wants to become a counselor and coach, inspiring other youngsters the way Dodd inspired him.

Meanwhile, his mother, who is struggling herself, is proud of her son and thankful that those around him never gave up. Vaught is thankful, too.

"You've got to go through the hard times. You gotta go through some crying, a lot of worrying. But once you get up the ladder, turn around and take a look at where you came from, say, 'Gosh, I came through all of that, and look where I am now,' " Bobby Vaught said.

"If you don't see anything, it means you didn't accomplish anything. But if you can turn around that ladder and say, 'Gosh, I came through all of that,' it makes you feel good."

And for teachers and coaches like Dodd, who struggle each day trying to reach out to youngsters who walk the thin line between success and failure, Bobby Vaught says thanks for making a difference.

"Please don't give up. We need those teachers so bad," he said. "They've got to hang in there for our sake, because without our teachers, we're lost. We're just not going to make it. It's that simple."

SNAPSHOT BIOGRAPHY

Bobby Vaught was born July 21, 1973, in Myrtle Beach, S.C. He moved to Kansas in 1980 and graduated from Wichita North High School. He attended Cloud County Community College in Concordia for three years and transferred in 1994 to Wichita State University. Years in Kansas: 14.

Taking Flight

Kelly Viets is living a dream in restoring a Travel Air plane

Lyndon

Kelly Viets loves history and the thrill of flight.

He's captured both in his airplane hangar near Pomona Lake in northeast Kansas.

"It is living a dream," he said. "It's going to be the supreme thrill of my life."

The dream is to restore an old Travel Air aircraft

that was originally built in the 1920s. Travel Air was an early Wichita airplane company founded by aviation pioneers Walter Beech, Clyde Cessna and Lloyd Stearman. The company later became Beech Aircraft Corp.

"Would you believe that I met the man who designed this?" Viets said, his smiling expression like a child's. "Lloyd Stearman came to fly in Lawrence, and I saw him there. So I guess I've been the luckiest kid to ever hang around an airport."

Lucky and smart. Viets is a rarity in engineering circles, a self-educated mechanical engineer who passed the professional engineering exam on his first try. He worked for 32 years as an engineering consultant and also earned his pilot's license.

His true love — and "the greatest hobby in the world," according to Viets — is flight.

"When you stand back — that is, get up in an airplane a couple thousand feet — you look down at what man has done, and it isn't all that bad. It's pretty darn wonderful," he said.

"And to be able to see more than just a couple of hundred feet either side of a highway, it fascinates

me. You get to see the changing of the seasons, which, to me, it's just marvelous.

"It gives you an uplift in your life."

Viets already has restored four old airplanes. But getting the Travel Air machine into the air is going to be this retired engineer's greatest accomplishment.

"You have to learn welding. You have to learn woodwork. You have to know about urethane varnishes," he said.

"It's like designing a power plant. You start with the first straight line, and then you start building on it."

Working in his hangar — chilly as a fridge in the winter, stuffy in the summer — Viets can spend hours talking about the plane. And everything he says, he punctuates with a broad smile.

"By the way, where on earth would you find a brand-new 1918 carburetor that has never been run?" he said, laughing.

"This old 90-horse engine would only turn 1,400 RPM on a good day, and I mean a good day. But that engine has more torque than a modern engine."

Viets' wife, Edna, whom he calls his childhood sweetheart, works right alongside him in the hangar, helping to assemble pieces and attach them to the aging aircraft. "She lived across the street, and I carried her books home in the first grade," Kelly Viets said. "We've been together ever since."

Kelly and Edna Viets are like many Kansas folks who enjoy aviation. They love it. They live it. And when their Travel Air machine is finished, there will be that moment when Kelly lifts it off the runway.

"At times, you get a little discouraged. At times you wonder if you'll get it all done," he said. "But it's like climbing a mountain, I guess. When you get to the top of it, it's a very exciting time."

For Viets, bringing past and present together in the skies over Pomona Lake is a glorious vision.

"Yes, you're seeing a kid living his dream," he said. "How could you be any happier?"

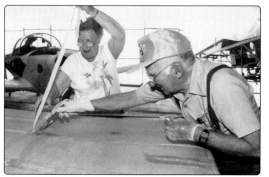

Edna and Kelly Viets work together to restore an old Travel Air aircraft in their hangar near Pomona Lake.

Kelly and Edna Viets display a picture of the Travel Air 2000 which they are restoring.

The Kennedy Connection

Robert Vinson thinks a mysterious flight he took in 1963 may be part of the assassination puzzle

Wichita

For more than 30 years, Robert Vinson has kept a secret.

It is the story of a mysterious plane ride, a mysterious landing, some mysterious passengers, and the assassination of President John F. Kennedy.

Vinson was in Washington, D.C., on the morning of Nov. 22, 1963, talking to a man behind the counter at Andrews Air Force Base, trying to hop a military flight back to his home base in Colorado Springs.

"You see that C-54 out there?" the man behind the counter told him, pointing toward a big cargo plane sitting on the tarmac.

"Yeah," Vinson said.

"It's going to Denver. Get on it."

Vinson did.

At about the same time, President Kennedy was preparing for a motorcade in Dallas.

On board the C-54 in Washington, Vinson thought it odd that neither the pilot nor co-pilot spoke to him. Also, there was no crew chief on board, a glaring absence because all Air Force flights required a crew chief. What's more, the designation on the tail of the aircraft was odd — not a normal Air Force insignia, Vinson said — and no one asked him to sign a logbook when he boarded the plane.

"There was no 'How are you doing?' No 'Nice to have you aboard.' Nothing," Vinson said. "Those guys were absolutely stone silent."

The plane took off and headed toward what Vinson assumed would be Lowry Air Force Base in Denver. But at 12:29 p.m., the pilot's voice came on the loudspeaker and made a terrible announcement.

"He said the president had been shot," Vinson said. "We were over Nebraska at the time, just a little south of Omaha, but right then we did a complete 180 and headed south."

The plane was on its way to Dallas. But it didn't land at an airport or military runway. It touched down on a dirt strip that Vinson said looked like an interstate road under construction.

"It could have been a dirt runway, but it looked more like a road," he said. Whatever it was, it wasn't a normal place for a large Air Force cargo plane to land.

"We came in real low and pretty hot, pretty fast, landed, never did shut the engines off," he said. "Pretty soon the co-pilot came back, unlatched the door, did not say anything to me, and two people boarded the aircraft. They were in off-white, beige type coveralls.

"I was sitting near the middle of the plane, because I like to fly near the wings. These men walked to the front, sat down right behind the cockpit and didn't speak to me or say anything."

Vinson said one of the men was tall, with Hispanic coloring and features. The other was Caucasian, with an average height and build. The plane was on the ground no more than five minutes before it took off again.

"I was real surprised. I mean, I didn't know what to think."

When the plane landed, the two mysterious passengers exited quickly, along with the pilot and co-pilot. Nobody spoke to Vinson. He didn't even know where he was.

"That was strange, very strange," Vinson said. "I couldn't understand why they were in such a rush. They just bailed out."

Vinson finally got off the plane, walked to a nearby building, and asked the man behind the counter where he was. "He said, 'This is Roswell Air Force Base, New Mexico.' " Vinson asked if he could catch a flight to Denver, and the airman told him the base was on "full alert," meaning no aircraft could come in or go out.

"I thought that was odd, too, because we had just landed," he said. "I felt like everyone else knew what was happening but me. . . . As far as I was concerned, it was the most unusual flight I had ever been on."

Over the next few months, Vinson was transferred to a new squadron, and his background was checked meticulously. Officials with the Federal Bureau of Investigation visited his neighborhood, asking friends and neighbors questions about Vinson and his wife, Roberta. Eventually, he was placed in a Central Intelligence Agency unit, and he and his wife were sworn to secrecy.

He told his story only after official documents concerning Kennedy's assassination were made public.

Was Vinson a witness to history, or was the mysterious plane ride only a coincidence? The answer might be tied to the unusual markings on the tail of the aircraft that Vinson took to Dallas. He said he later found that they indicated the plane belonged to the CIA.

"I feel that there is a connection. My wife feels there is a connection," he said. "I'm not what you would call an assassination buff, but I do believe there was some kind of conspiracy."

The Warren Commission, which investigated Kennedy's assassination, dismissed a report that there may have been a getaway plane waiting, as well as reports that men in beige overalls were seen on the grassy knoll overlooking Dealy Plaza the day the president was shot. Nevertheless, Kennedy theorists say the assassination is a complex, mysterious puzzle.

And Robert Vinson's secret could be a piece.

SNAPSHOT BIOGRAPHY

Robert Vinson was born Dec. 12, 1928, in Headland, Ala. He joined the U.S. Army in May 1946 and served until November 1947. In 1948 he joined the U.S. Air Force and held several positions, including one with the Central Intelligence Agency. He retired from the military in 1966. Shortly after retiring, he moved to Wichita, where he worked as an accountant and then as an administrative assistant and supervisor in the city Public Works Department. He has a degree in business administration from Kansas Newman College. He and his wife, Roberta, were married Dec. 18, 1959, in Amarillo, Texas. He has two children and two stepchildren. Years in Kansas: 27.

Robert Vinson has unusual memories of the day President John F. Kennedy was assassinated.

The Guy With the Giraffes

Charles Walker is a successful businessman — and a zookeeper of sorts

Salina

Charles Walker never went into business to get rich, he says. He went into business to keep from being poor.

Whatever the reason, Walker overcame poverty and the limitations of an eighth-grade education to become chairman and chief executive officer of Blue Beacon International and Power Vac Inc., Salina-based companies with about 2,200 employees on the payroll.

"It just turned out that I did pretty well," Walker said.

But although people in business circles may know Walker for his rags-to-riches success story, thousands of area kindergartners know him as the guy with the giraffes.

In 1980 Walker bought a 320-acre ranch west of Salina, built a house on the property, bought a herd of cattle and kept going. As is the case with most of Walker's business ventures, Rolling Hills Ranch boomed.

Today, the ranch spans 11,000 acres and houses more than 40 species of animals, including zebras, camels, snow leopards and giraffes.

Recently, it teamed with Manhattan's Sunset Zoological Park to form a Wildlife Conservation and Research Cooperative to breed and study endangered species. By 1995, the ranch hopes to have several varieties of Asian deer, cheetahs, chimpanzees and a breeding pair of black rhinoceroses which, when not roaming in their reinforced enclosure, will live in a state-of-the-art, $150,000 barn.

The partnership between Walker's ranch and the Manhattan zoo is the first of its kind in Kansas.

And overseeing everything is a down-home guy who wears a cowboy hat, flies his own company jets and helicopters and, with the help of 10 full-time cowboys, still runs about 800 head of black baldy cattle.

"I learned very early to surround myself with the very best quality people, to learn from them and to share with them," he said. "I've had good people, and I've worked hard."

In 1985 Walker was named Small Businessman of the Year by the Wichita district office of the Small Business Administration. His companies manufacture industrial cleaning devices and chemicals and operate truck stops, truck washes and convenience stores across the United States and in Canada.

But Walker's true love is the ranch. He still lives on the property and spends most of his time there. And until recently, when the ranch was closed for construction of the wildlife conservation area, he loved taking area youngsters around the park and showing them his animals.

"It's interesting for them, and it's educational at the same time," he said. "I think they really love it."

It wasn't always that way. When Rolling Hills Ranch first opened, Walker's main attraction was a herd of 130 Belgian horses. Actually, that was Walker's *only* attraction.

"For those little kids, one horse looked pretty much like the others, so they got bored after about 10," he said. "I threw in some zebras after a while, and they really liked that."

Then he threw in some cougars, lions, black bears, camels, llamas, ostriches, kangaroos and giraffes, and Rolling Hills Ranch became a member of the American Association of Zoos, Parks and Aquariums.

"I just grew to appreciate the animals, and to love them, and I kept buying and getting more and more," Walker said.

Before its partnership with the Manhattan zoo, the ranch was open for tour groups by appointment only. When it reopens as the Rolling Hills Ranch Wildlife Conservation Area in 1995, it will be open to the public and have regular hours, much like a normal zoo, Walker said.

Schoolchildren will probably still visit the ranch by the busload, and Walker will continue to get thank-you letters and crayon pictures of Slim, the giraffe that eats out of your hand.

"It gives you a nice feeling to see all those little kids and their parents. Most of them have never seen a camel or a kangaroo or an ostrich," Walker said. "This teaches them something, and it's fun."

So the Kansas boy who started a business to keep from being poor has grown rich. Very rich, indeed.

Camels are among the many animals on Charles Walker's ranch.

Charles Walker shares a treat with one of the giraffes on his ranch.

Velma Lunt Wallace was born in Wichita. She graduated from Wichita North High School and earned a degree from Wichita Business College. She married Dwane L. Wallace on Sept. 8, 1941, in Forestville, Md. She has four children.

Velma Wallace in her office. Dwane Wallace's picture is in the background.

Coming Into Her Own

Velma Wallace, finding an inner strength, moves her life in a new direction

Wichita

She is one of Wichita's most well-known women, but for years she lived outside the spotlight, in the shadows.

Velma Wallace was the wife of the late Dwane Wallace, an aviation pioneer who brought Cessna Aircraft Corp. through five decades of growth. And although Dwane Wallace and his career were bigger than life, Velma tried her best to avoid the spotlight.

"I didn't like it at all," she said with a chuckle. "I went to the Cessna meetings because I had to go. But I didn't like it because of, well, a lack of confidence. Because I had never been put in those positions before, so it was very new and very frightening to me."

Wallace was the daughter of a Sedgwick County dairy farmer, a man who struggled to support his family. The riches and notoriety she later attained through her husband's successful career were not things she was accustomed to having. Growing up, she had almost nothing.

"We had no plumbing, no running water. I dressed behind a potbellied stove with a sheet around it," she said.

And even in her early years, she didn't like attention. "I was a very shy little girl, and when people would come to the house, I would run and hide."

Then, in 1941, she married Dwane Wallace, a Kansas farm boy who was destined to be an aviation legend. She loved him deeply.

"He confided, I would say, everything in me," she said.

But as Cessna grew and Dwane Wallace became a household name, Velma Wallace withdrew. She hated the limelight. And, like many other people whose spouses become famous, she found that people sometimes didn't care about her.

"People probably won't take this the way it was meant, but to always have people talking, 'Dwane does this. Dwane, Dwane, Dwane.' And I was a nonentity," she said.

"Perhaps they didn't mean it that way, but he was who he was, and I was proud of him, and I loved him, and it will always be that way. . . . It was difficult."

For years, Velma Wallace kept the secret — loving her husband, hating her insecurities. She suffered in silence.

"It was so difficult sometimes, I wasn't sure I could handle it," she said. "And I would have gone for help, but that would not have been right. Dwane would not have approved."

Velma Wallace discusses aviation photographs. Her late husband, Dwane, was an aviation pioneer.

Several years ago, Dwane Wallace died after a short illness. Velma's life almost came apart, until one of her daughters persuaded her to get help. She hopes that by talking about her experiences, she will help other people in similar situations.

"I would have gone into the depths of depression if I had not had help, and I highly recommend it."

Through counseling, Velma Wallace discovered she had personal strengths that even she wasn't aware of. The insecurities that had haunted her for a lifetime faded away. She became her own person.

"I've set some goals for myself, things that I want to accomplish, and I think, health permitting, I'm going to accomplish them."

One of her goals is to share her family's wealth and good fortune with the rest of the community. Most recently, she made headlines as the person who donated $10 million to build a new children's museum and science center on the banks of the Arkansas River in downtown Wichita.

She intends to stay involved in life. Until June 1994, when she sold her personal plane, she even continued to enjoy the freedom of flight.

"It's nice to be up in the wild blue yonder and look down on the beautiful earth," she said. "And you wonder how there can be so much trouble."

Facing the Crowd

Comedian and hairdresser Bucky Walters loves to make 'em laugh

Wichita

To know Bucky Walters is to laugh.

"They're wholesome. They're simple. They're boring," Walters said, imitating a certain well-known television personality. "They're Hatteberg's People!"

Nice to know someone can make fun of himself.

Then again, Walters, a Wichita hairdresser during business hours and a renowned actor, comedian and political impersonator the rest of the time, makes fun of just about everybody.

Who else would attend his 35th high school reunion dressed not only in drag, but as Kansas Gov. Joan Finney? Who else can assume the deep voice of Sen. Bob Dole one minute — "I know it, you know it, the American people know it" — and the nasal twang of former Gov. Mike Hayden the next?

"I remember when I went to New York and represented Kansas at Bloomingdale's," Hayden, er, Walters said. "I'll never forget it, because I came riding in on that horse, and I know I made an impression, because the president of Bloomingdale's himself helped me down off the horse and told me I was everything he'd ever imagined in a Kansas governor.

"And I thought that was naaahhce."

Walters began his show business career in the late 1950s, when he formed his own rock 'n' roll band, The Premiers. One year, the band went on the road with "The Johnny Cash Show," a traveling variety show that featured the famous country singer. For several more years, they played dances and nightclubs in the Wichita area.

"Back then, rock 'n' roll was such a magic word," Walters said. "You could put up a poster that just said 'rock 'n' roll,' without the name of the band or anything, and people just flocked."

Eventually, though, he thought he should get serious about a career. Or maybe just his parents thought he should get serious.

"I started doing hair mainly because my parents were asking me to do something. I'd come back home, and it was like, 'When are you going to do something?' So I went to beauty school just to get them off my back."

Meanwhile, the agent of The Premiers persuaded Walters to take some of his informal comedy routines, which he usually performed backstage or in corners at parties, and share them with the public. So for a short time, Walters played some clubs in Wichita.

But these weren't comedy clubs, if you know what we mean.

"They didn't really have comedy clubs back then. All they had was strip clubs," he said. "So I'd do one or two quick one-liners, and it was, 'Let's bring out the vivacious Yolanda.'

"You know, I'd always hear the girls laughing in back. I think they liked me. But I never heard them laughing in the front."

Walters continued his increasingly successful career as a hairstylist and saved the comedy routines for friends.

Then one evening at a party, the director of "Comedia," an annual stage show that poked fun at local, state and national news-makers, asked Walters if he would like to audition. Ever since, his name is printed beside the phrase "Wichita hairdresser and comedian."

Walters is perhaps best known for his impersonations of Kansas politicians, especially Hayden and Finney, and he performs often at banquets, campaign activities and roasts. He is also a regular performer in "Gridiron," an annual comedy production written and produced by local journalists.

Although his comedic career is generally a sideline activity, Walters said that making people laugh is his primary passion.

"Oh, yeah, I need to be facing the crowd, not sitting in it," he said. "I've felt all along that people should be watching me. I can go to other shows and appreciate them, but I want to be up on stage with them."

Eventually even politicians who are the subject of Walters' scathing impersonations have learned to respect and appreciate his special talent. That includes Hayden.

"I know that the only reason you're having me here today," the former governor said during one of his campaign fund-raisers, "is so I can do my Bucky Walters impression."

SNAPSHOT BIOGRAPHY

R.G. "Bucky" Walters was born April 6, 1939, in Wichita. He graduated from East High School and attended Wichita State University. He spent several years touring as the bassist and front man for his band, The Premiers, before attending cosmetology school and beginning his career as a hairdresser. Years in Kansas: 55.

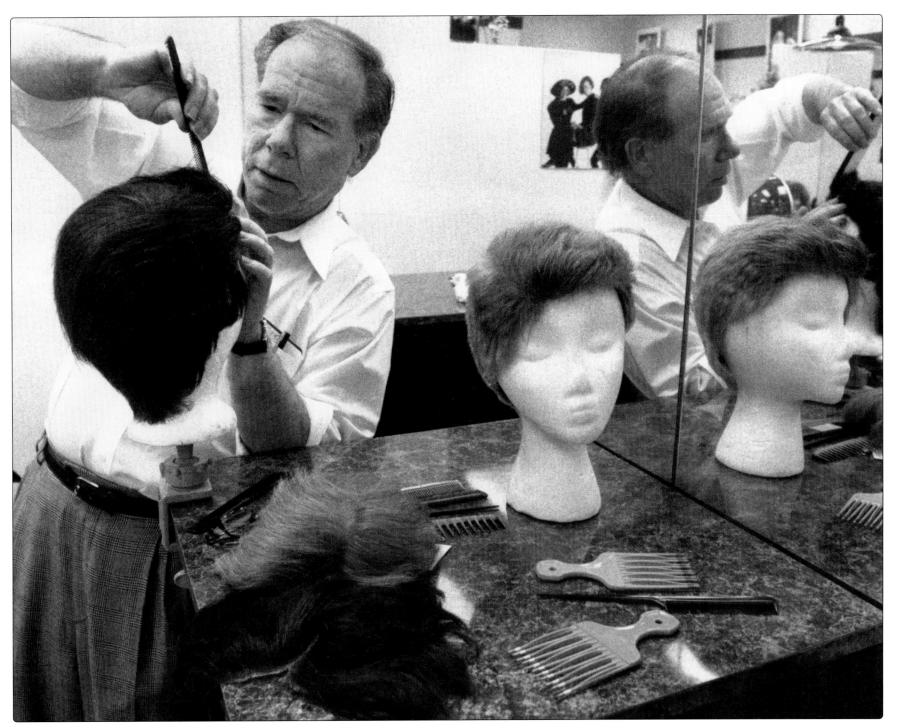

Bucky Walters prepares his wigs for a performance. He performs often at banquets, campaign activities and at roasts.

SNAPSHOT BIOGRAPHY

Robert Watson was born Feb. 25, 1895, in Maryville, Mo. He was drafted into the U.S. Army in 1917 and discharged in 1919, after being wounded. After returning home, he earned his bachelor's degree in education from Northwest Missouri State University and his master's in school administration from the University of Missouri. He worked as a teacher and school superintendent for 20 years, during which he met his wife, Elvira. They were married June 1, 1924, and had three children. She died in 1987. Watson joined the American Red Cross in 1942 and served as field director in several military camps during World War II. He moved to Kansas in 1945 to work at the Veterans Administration hospital in Wichita. Years in Kansas: 49.

Robert Watson displays his medal commemorating the 75th anniversary of World War I.

Veteran

A soldier in World War I, Robert Watson worked for the Red Cross during World War II

Wichita

In 1988, to commemorate the 70th anniversary of the end of World War I, the Veterans Administration hospital in Wichita invited all surviving World War I veterans to attend a ceremony at the hospital. Thirty-nine veterans attended.

In 1993, to commemorate the war's 75th anniversary, the hospital extended the same invitation. Only 13 vets attended that time, most in stretchers or wheelchairs. Since then, four of those men have died.

But not Robert Watson.

Watson, a sharp, witty, vibrant 99-year-old, is not only alive and walking, he still mows his lawn in the summer, rakes leaves in the fall and rides his stationary bike about 100 miles a week.

Watson's life is a lesson in hard work, perseverance and faith.

As a young man drafted into service during World War I, Watson experienced things most people only read about in history books. He suffered a bullet wound to his left leg early in his tour of duty, but as soon as it healed, he was sent back to the front lines.

One day he was advancing with a group of soldiers when German troops spotted them and started firing.

"I suppose they killed 15 or 20 of our men, just slaughtered them. I was able to escape without any injuries," he said. "Those are things you just can't forget."

Not long after, he was crossing a stream in France when he was hit with shrapnel in five different places. He survived, but he spent several days in a field hospital and was eventually transferred to another hospital. But even in the midst of tragedy, Watson managed to keep his sense of humor.

"One day they told us we would be transferred to another hospital. And we were told to take our old pajamas off, because they were bringing clean pajamas for all of us," he said. "When they brought the new pajamas and started scattering them around, there wasn't enough for everybody."

They gave Watson an extra blanket and sent him on. When Watson arrived at the new hospital, a nurse was instructed to check each patient's injuries and assign him to the proper ward.

"When she got to me, I just wasn't accustomed to a lady throwing the blanket back when I didn't have any pajamas on," Watson said, chuckling.

"She said, 'What's wrong?' And I said, 'I don't have anything on, that's what.'"

His injuries took about five months to heal, after which he received an honorable discharge from the Army. Among his collection of military medals is the Silver Star, the Purple Heart with oak-leaf cluster, the victory medal with four battle bars, and a citation from his division commander.

After the war, he earned his bachelor's and master's degrees in education and served as a teacher and superintendent throughout his home state of Missouri. He also spent eight years as a farmer, tending about 85 acres of wheat, corn and oats near King City, Mo.

Watson joined the American Red Cross in 1942 and served as field director in several military camps during World War II. After the war, he continued with the Red Cross, helping veterans file claims for military disability. He moved to Wichita in 1945 to work at the Veterans Administration hospital.

He retired from the Red Cross in 1960, but continued for many years as an active volunteer. In early 1994, Elizabeth Dole, director of the American Red Cross, awarded Watson a certificate of appreciation for his years of service.

"I didn't even know I was getting anything," he said. "And I got to the dinner, and there she was. It was a true honor."

Watson says his secret to long life could be his healthy appetite. "I never did care much for chicken. I had to kill too many as a kid." Or it could be his calendar full of banquets and church meetings. Or maybe a clue is in his kitchen, where a refrigerator he bought in 1948 is still working fine.

"Some things," he said, "just last."

Watson keeps in shape by pedaling his exercise bike every day.

Traveling a Rocky Road

Collecting stones is Henry Westfahl's passion

Arlington

It's a small farm, Henry Westfahl's place in the wide open spaces of western Reno County. And from a distance, it looks like an average farm — barns, fences, even a cattle pen out back.

But look closer, and you'll see the difference.

There aren't any cows in that cattle pen, for instance. Only piles of rocks. No saddles or bridles in the work shed. Just rocks. And in the building that used to be the washroom? You guessed it. More rocks.

Henry Westfahl is spending his retirement with rocks, and he loves every colorful, mysterious, glistening day of it.

"The wife, she likes to watch the soap operas in the afternoons," he said, walking slowly toward the shed behind his house. "So that's when I come out here and work."

Born in Haven in 1906, Westfahl began collecting rocks almost by accident, after Dust Bowl winds uncovered hundreds of arrowheads once hidden in western Kansas. He and his fiance, Mattie Lee, would spend hours hunting the Indian treasures, which Henry kept in a box. The couple married in Liberal in 1930 and moved to their current home in Arlington, and they've been collecting rocks together ever since.

Henry calls them nature's art.

"This is natural. You take your paintings, and that's artificial," he said. "But you take and saw a rock, and that there is a rock that's been formed millions of years ago. And you don't know how it was formed — that's the funny part or the great part about it."

His collection includes pink salt from Kanopolis, petrified wood from Wyoming, melted sand from the first atomic bomb test in White Sands, N.M., silicon silver from California and even a piece of man-made rock — a chunk of concrete from the Berlin Wall.

"I've been pretty much everywhere," he said. "All the states except Connecticut and Rhode Island. People send me rocks or give 'em to me. I keep everything."

He places his collection carefully inside glass display cases or on shelves that fill his work shed. For each specimen, there is a typed or handwritten label showing the name of the rock and where it was found. But Westfahl rarely needs labels.

"Take this one here," he said, handing a visitor a reddish-brown chunk of rock. "Smell it. What does it smell like?"

Well, a rock.

"What does it look like?"

Looks like a rock, too. The outside is bumpy and hard, like concrete. And the inside — revealed after Westfahl cuts and polishes it — is red, orange and slate gray, all melted together like the inside of a glass marble.

"Yeah, it looks like a rock, don't it?" he said, laughing. "That's carponite. It's petrified dinosaur dung."

It's Westfahl's favorite trick. When groups of youngsters visit his place on class field trips or as part of 4-H excursions, he passes around the chunk of Jurassic history and watches their expressions when he reveals the secret.

"They go 'Eewww,'" he said, wrinkling his nose like a child faced with a plateful of lima beans. "And I just laugh and tell 'em, 'Now, you see, rocks can be anything.'"

Some folks think Westfahl is crazy, spending hard-earned retirement with a pickax and a burlap sack, digging in the dirt and licking dirty rocks "to see how they'd look when they're polished up." Once a farmer and rancher, he retired more than a decade ago when the work became too tiring. Now he collects rocks instead of eggs, cuts blocks of stone instead of wheat.

It's not your typical Reno County pastime, but he doesn't care. In fact, he said, those rocks actually keep him from going loony.

"When you quit work, you gotta have a hobby," he said. "If you just set down in a rocking chair and watch television, why, you'll just last about two or three years, and they'll have you out on the hill.

"There's a lot of happiness right there," he said, motioning toward the palmwood, agate and "Apache tears" rocks that fill old mayonnaise and peanut butter jars on his shelf. The rocks take months to sand and polish, but he takes it one day at a time.

"I wouldn't trade 'em for a million dollars. No sir."

Henry Westfahl has bins of rocks from all over the world.

Opposite: Westfahl displays a fossil fish rock from Wyoming.

S N A P S H O T   B I O G R A P H Y

Henry Westfahl was born March 23, 1906, in Haven. He and his wife, Mattie Lee, married on June 1, 1930, in Liberal and finally settled in Arlington. They have one son. Years in Kansas: 88.

"This is natural. You take your paintings, and that's artificial. But you take and saw a rock, and that there is a rock that's been formed millions of years ago. And you don't know how it was formed — that's the funny part or the great part about it."

Secure in Their Spot

Winston and Eva Wheeler can find whatever you want; they have what they want

Larkinburg

"**H**ow are ya?" Winston Wheeler greets the man who has just parked his pickup on the gravel driveway.

"I'm doing just fine," the visitor answers. "I need a couple rolls of your second-grade barbed wire."

"I got it."

You bet he's got it. He's got just about everything you'd ever need. And although Wheeler's Hardware might look to the average customer like 16 acres of sheds, farm machinery and Kansas countryside, in no particular order, Wheeler knows just where to find what you're looking for.

And he does it — get this! — without a computer.

"That would be my only hope, that we never go to computer," Wheeler said. "My biggest problem with companies we buy from is their computers. It seems to be the alibi for any error."

So Wheeler and his wife, Eva, operate one of the state's largest hardware stores the old-fashioned way. The way the Wheelers and their customers like it. With the help of their sons, they also run a farm and ranch.

"Everybody knows where everything is at, and it comes and goes," said Eva, who helps keep the books for the hardware store. "If we're out, we reorder."

"Eva's got this thing down," Winston said.

"It's all right there," she said, gesturing toward a pile of folders on her desk. "Comes in, goes out."

Simple strategy, simple town. Wheeler Hardware is in Larkinburg — or, rather, the store *is* Larkinburg. A church, a few houses, several barking dogs and an occasional mule make up the unincorporated community about eight miles east of Holton.

People travel hundreds of miles to this big store in this tiny town to buy gaskets, bearings and other replacement parts for pooped-out farm machinery. Just the other day, a man came all the way from Liberty, Mo., to buy a new mower.

"We've been around 40 years, so a lot of people know about us," Eva said. "They come from, well, just about everywhere."

Perhaps Wheeler's hammers, shovels, nuts and bolts are better than anyone else's. Or maybe, just maybe, those

Winston Wheeler has in stock just about everything you would ever need.

customers come for the service.

"It's peaceful. It's good country," Winston said. "Good neighborhood. Genuine people. And I enjoy the customers, I really do."

Here in the country, time is not a problem. Winston has been known to spend an hour finding just the right piece of equipment.

"We need one more bearing," he said, walking down one aisle of his store, which is stacked from floor to ceiling with miscellaneous gadgets. "Number sixty-seven-oh-forty-eight."

He'll find it. Eventually. Because Winston Wheeler knows that everything a guy could possibly want is right here in Larkinburg, right here at home. And if he had the chance, he'd do it all over again.

"I'd pick the same girl, I'd want to be in the same location, and I'd want the family just like it is," he said. "Anybody can do what I do. It's just that you learn where stuff is at."

SNAPSHOT BIOGRAPHY

Winston Wheeler was born Oct. 14, 1924, in Atchison. Eva Wheeler was born May 13, 1926, in Fort Madison, Iowa. They met at Atchison County Community High School and were married June 15, 1944, in Larkinburg, where they now live and work. They have three children. Years in Kansas: Winston 69, Eva 63.

Winston and Eva Wheeler wait on a full complement of customers in their hardware store in Larkinburg. Wheeler's Hardware covers 16 acres.

Zuzu Forever

Karolyn Grimes Wilkerson will always be known for her part in 'It's a Wonderful Life'

Stilwell

When postal carriers in Stilwell get letters addressed, "Zuzu, Stilwell, KS," they know right where to take them.

Her name is Karolyn Grimes Wilkerson, a 54-year-old woman living in a suburb of Kansas City with a houseful of dogs, cats and Hollywood memorabilia. But to the thousands of people who have seen "It's a Wonderful Life," who have wiped away sentimental tears when the golden-haired girl tells her father, George Bailey of Bedford Falls, that "Every time a bell rings, an angel gets his wings," she will always be Zuzu.

Not once during the filming of the movie did she ever imagine it would become a classic. But today, after surviving more than the average share of tragedies in her own life, Wilkerson realizes why the film means so much to so many people.

"I can draw from that movie myself, and it even inspires me to touch other people's lives in good ways, if I can," she said.

Wilkerson was born in Hollywood, Calif., and became an actress at age 3, after her father was drafted to fight in World War II. Her family needed the money. Her first role was a bit part in the movie "Pardon My Past," starring Fred MacMurray.

In later years, she worked with Cary Grant, Gabby Hayes and Bing Crosby. She was only 6 when she landed the role of Zuzu, the little girl who watched her father, played by Jimmy Stewart, discover how one man's life touches so many others.

Wilkerson left Hollywood at 14, following her mother's death. A year later, her father died in an automobile accident, and she was sent to live with an aunt and uncle in Missouri.

She didn't return to California until last year, when the Target discount store chain, as part of a holiday promotion, sponsored a "Bailey kid reunion." The company hired Wilkerson and the three other former actors who portrayed Stewart's children to tour the country, talking with fans and signing autographs.

During the tour, people told Wilkerson and the other actors how the 1946 film affected their lives.

One couple's wedding rings were engraved with the quote, "I will love you 'til the day I die" — the phrase that young Mary whispers into George Bailey's deaf ear. Another man told them he was thinking of committing suicide until he saw the movie and, like George Bailey, reconsidered. Others said they named their dogs, their cats, even their children, after Zuzu.

And in case you've always wondered where the name came from . . .

"There's a scene where George comes home from his escapade, after he finds out that he really loves his family, and he dashes up the stairs to greet me and says, 'Zuzu! Zuzu, my little gingersnap!' Well, that's what it is," Wilkerson said. On her shelf at home is an antique cookie tin — Zuzu brand gingersnaps.

Late in 1993 Wilkerson visited with other members of the "Wonderful Life" cast and crew in Indiana, Pa., Stewart's hometown, which held a three-day festival and reunion. Again, she was flooded with old memories and new stories.

"It was so heartwarming, to see how this movie touched so many people's lives," she said. "And at the same time, it has given me back my past, which I thought was irretrievable."

Although her travels have taught Wilkerson that she is part of Hollywood history, they also convinced her that Kansas is home.

"Even though I had a wonderful time, my heart will always be here," she said. "The people are so genuine, sincere and honest, not superficial. They're really true friends, people you can count on.

"Kansas is my Bedford Falls."

SNAPSHOT BIOGRAPHY

Karolyn Grimes Wilkerson was born July 4, 1940, in Hollywood, Calif. Her mother died when she was 14. Her father was killed in a car accident a year later, and she moved to Missouri to live with an aunt and uncle. As an adult, she moved to Overland Park, a suburb of Kansas City. She and her late husband, Mike, were married July 19, 1969, in Kansas City, Mo. He died in May 1994. She has two children from a previous marriage, one child and three stepchildren from her second marriage. Years in Kansas: 26.

Karolyn Grimes Wilkerson was Zuzu in the "rose petal" scene with Jimmy Stewart in "It's a Wonderful Life."

Apple of Their Eye

Mike and Elaine Williamson are trying to make their dream of an orchard come true

Lyons

Mike and Elaine Williamson are passionate about two things: raising healthy children and raising tasty apples.

And funny enough, the activities fit together nicely.

"The apple orchard is our hope and our dream for a family-based lifestyle," Mike Williamson said. "The whole idea of buying an apple orchard and living there was to provide a home and a business where we could raise and home-educate our children."

The Williamsons — Mike, Elaine and their children, Katie, Betony, Willow, J.J. and Pippin — are living a dream. They own and operate the Sandhill Prairie Farm, a 15-acre apple orchard in central Kansas.

Mike and Elaine fell in love with orchards more than a decade ago, while Mike was teaching school and working toward his master's degree at Middlebury College in Middlebury, Vt. While he studied the biological aspects of fruit and strategies for making apple orchards more productive, she learned how to make cider and apple butter.

Their original plan was for Mike to attend veterinary school. But one evening, over a dinner of chicken-fried steak, they got to thinking.

"I thought, 'Wouldn't it be great to buy a place in the Sandhills, a place that we knew very well, and just raise apples and asparagus and raspberries and strawberries?' " Mike said.

A few weeks later, Elaine's father, a banker in Lyons, called to tell them that a 15-acre orchard was for sale just outside Lyons. The Williamsons couldn't decide whether the news was fate, dumb luck or divine intervention, but they got a government loan and moved back to Kansas.

They took over the orchard and moved the family into a converted barn on the property. Although the couple was excited and hopeful about their prospects as fruit farmers, they also knew their dream wouldn't come easy.

And it hasn't. First, they learned that the orchard's former owner had planted full-size trees in spaces designed for dwarf trees. Consequently, the trees were too cramped to grow and produce fruit, so the Williamsons had to thin out the orchard, getting rid of almost half of the trees.

Then, five years of drought conditions and severe Kansas weather, combined with the couple's trial-and-error style of farming, turned the Williamsons' beautiful dream into something of a nightmare.

"We had a terrible hailstorm, and we went from a full crop to no crop in fifteen minutes," Mike said. "That's real sobering."

Still, they kept hoping, and they never forgot what they love about their unique lifestyle. Their twin boys, in fact, are named after two of the most popular apple varieties from the turn of the century — Jonathan and Pippin.

"When you've filled the air with apple blossoms, and millions of blooms and petals are flying everywhere — that's what's so wonderful about being in the apple orchard," Mike said. "Once you graft them, once you prune them and train them, you're hooked. That's all it is, I'm actually hooked on apples."

Unfortunately, apples haven't paid the bills, so Mike runs a laundry and dry-cleaning business in Lyons that once belonged to his father and grandfather. Elaine stays home with the children, teaching them math, reading and a few lessons they wouldn't learn in the city.

"I'll be standing up at the kitchen window, doing piles of dishes, and I look out over this and hear the wind blowing over the cottonwoods and watch the ducks on the pond," she said. "And I see my kids playing and running around.

"Our kids have an extraordinary amount of freedom out here, and after years of having kids around, I know that that's what they need."

For now, Sandhill Prairie Farm is on a hiatus, waiting for batches of new trees to grow and bloom and produce sweet, juicy apples. Eventually, Mike wants to develop an organic farm that would capitalize on the area's unusual geography and weather, rather than fight it.

"We've pursued our dream, and we've made mistakes, and that's OK. We've learned a lot about ourselves in the meantime," Mike said. "So, you see? We haven't lost at all."

SNAPSHOT BIOGRAPHY

Mike Williamson was born Nov. 7, 1955, in Lyons. He and his wife, Elaine, who is also from Lyons, met in high school and were married June 3, 1978. Both attended the University of Kansas, where Mike earned his bachelor of science in botany and Elaine earned a bachelor of arts in visual arts. They spent four years in Middlebury, Vt., where Mike earned his master's in biology from Middlebury College. They have five children. Years in Kansas: Mike 34, Elaine 33.

Mike and Elaine Williamson and their family enjoy the apple blossoms in their orchard near Lyons.

Almost a Curse

Basil and Evelyn Wilson's pursuit of quality in furniture has its price

Haven

It hasn't been easy for Basil and Evelyn Wilson to follow their dream.

"I don't know what a normal marriage is like," Evelyn Wilson said. "But my husband has had to work about 80 hours a week, so I've had to do a lot of things by myself."

That's because Basil Wilson doesn't just make furniture; he creates works of art. And that takes time.

The tables, chairs, desks and dressers on the showroom floor of Basil Wilson & Co. in Haven, formerly Yoder Furniture, are museum-quality heirlooms. Antiques without the age. And crafting them by hand is what Wilson has worked a lifetime to do.

"It takes a lot, and I think that's why I love what I do," he said. "If I tell somebody I'll give them this quality, and a little extra, I feel good."

Wilson started by building cradles, rocking horses and other small projects, mostly for relatives and friends. He discovered he had natural talent — he calls it "a gift from God" — and others began to appreciate his unique craftsmanship. As a contractor working for architects and designers in Wichita, he developed a reputation for building beautiful spiral staircases and other decorative woodwork.

When he founded Yoder Furniture, he sold 100 handmade chairs without ever having one on a showroom floor.

"I did a lot of verbal descriptions and arm waving to show people the kind of product we could make for them," he said.

Wilson's designs are based on classics, with added details and finishing that make them unique. One style of chair he makes, the Windsor, dates back to 14th-century England.

Unlike much of today's mass-marketed, factory-produced furniture, Wilson's products are crafted entirely by hand with the finest materials, and they're built to last. (One chair on his showroom floor was thrown out of a truck at 55 miles an hour — by accident, of course — and it suffered only a few scratches.) They are made from oak, pine, cedar or walnut, woods whose colors grow richer and deeper by the year.

Consequently, his prices are higher than those of other companies — $500 to $600 for an average chair and thousands of dollars for bigger items, such as tables and desks. But that doesn't mean Wilson is wealthy; on the contrary, higher prices mean fewer sales, and the Wilsons often struggle to keep their family afloat.

"It's almost a curse," Basil Wilson said. "There have been a lot of times that our family's phone has been shut off. There are a lot of low periods we go through."

During those times, he takes temporary work with area contractors but returns to his shop in the evening and on weekends to make furniture. It's part of his mission to increase people's appreciation for heirloom-quality furniture.

"I've kind of had to educate people a little bit," he said. "We've been programmed by our society for the immediate, for now. People don't look for workmanship or longevity, but that's the way our country was built.

"We feel, as a company, that

we would like to create heirlooms of tomorrow from the day they go out of here."

Melding into the Amish community of Yoder, and now in Haven, the Wilson family shares that dream. Basil Jr. and Chloe help their father in the workshop and display area, and Evelyn Wilson keeps the books.

Basil Wilson works, quietly and steadily, as sawdust gathers on his workshop floor. Running his hand over the back of a newly built chair, he thinks of the old masters, and he hopes his old-fashioned work ethic and appreciation for quality will be an example for his children.

"I know how big a cost it has been to me, as a father and as a provider, and I have to believe that it will be worth it," he said. "I just want to teach my kids that it's worth going the extra mile in life."

SNAPSHOT BIOGRAPHY

Basil Wilson was born Sept. 24, 1949, in Wichita. He dropped out of high school but earned his general equivalency diploma while serving in the U.S. Marine Corps in the late 1960s. He and his wife, Evelyn, who was also born in Wichita, were married June 17, 1972. The couple spent several years in Minnesota, where Basil began his woodworking business. They later moved to Yoder, where they founded Yoder Furniture. They recently moved the store, now called Basil Wilson & Co., to Haven. Years in Kansas: 40.

Basil Wilson creates the "heirlooms of tomorrow" in his wood-furniture shop in Haven.

Wes Winters belts out a song during a performance at the Westin Crown Center in Kansas City, Mo.

Piano Man

Wes Winters plays it by ear, since he never studied music

Kansas City, Mo.

It's a Saturday night at the Westin Crown Center, one of Kansas City's most exclusive hotels, and Wes Winters knows just what those two lovebirds in the corner want to hear.

"Unforgettable . . . that's what you are. . . . "

So, too, is Winters. A self-taught and accomplished musician and singer, Winters delights lis-

---

SNAPSHOT BIOGRAPHY

Wes Winters was born Dec. 11, 1964, in Hays. He moved with his family to Olathe, where he graduated from Olathe North High School. He attended one semester at Johnson County Community College. He now lives in the historic Westport area of Kansas City, Mo. Years in Kansas: 25.

---

teners with his boyish good looks and seemingly endless repertoire. He is a piano man extraordinaire, and some say his weekly performance is one of the best shows in Kansas City.

"If you've got a big, nice crowd of people, you need to grab them with the very first song when you go out there," Winters said. "And if you grab them, you've got them the rest of the night."

Winters was born in Hays but moved to the Kansas City area when he was a youngster. It was there, you'll probably think, where he took those years of piano lessons, which led to those years of study at the world's finest universities, which led to the way he glides his hands so effortlessly across the piano keys.

He did study music, didn't he?

"Well, no, I didn't," Winters said. By now,

though, he's used to the question.

"They'll say, 'Did you take piano lessons?' and I say, 'No, I play by ear.' And then they go, 'Oh, I hate you.' That's usually what comes out of their mouth."

In Winters' mind — and in his ears — are the words and music to more than 1,000 songs, everything from "Orange Blossom Special" and "Mack the Knife" to "Boogie Woogie Bugle Boy" and that old lounge-lizard favorite, "New York, New York." At the Westin Crown Center, "Kansas City" is another popular request.

Dressed in a snazzy white tuxedo and silver-sequined bow tie, he plays the piano and synthesizer without any written music — just raw talent.

On one Saturday night, one couple nodded and tapped their feet to the music, then headed to the dance floor when Winters started singing "Under the Boardwalk."

"It's a gift," he said. "I really do believe that."

When the music stops, Wes Winters is just another resident of Kansas City's historic Westport area, enjoying time at home with his pet Rottweiler. But the music seldom stops.

Besides his regular shows at the Crown Center, Winters has spent the past 15 years performing in numerous clubs, lounges, hotels, corporate parties and theatrical shows. He has played in Dallas, Cincinnati, Las Vegas, Palm Springs and, most recently, in Branson, Mo. In 1991 he was named "Live!

Entertainer of the Year" for the Kansas City area. He also has been the featured male performer for three years at the annual Miss Missouri beauty pageant.

"I want to be the best at something," he said. "I want to be something that people really want to come and hear. I want to be the best entertainer that they've ever seen."

If the applause is any indication, he already is.

Winters, right, meets with his manager, Frank Dorcy, during a break.

Reaching for the Stars

John and Mary Wright's Old Mill Tasty Shop is a forerunner

Wichita

Before there was Old Town, there was the Old Mill.

The Old Mill Tasty Shop, a little ice cream and sandwich joint on East Douglas in downtown Wichita, was opened by Otto and Erne Woermke in 1932, when Wichita was barely on the map, and downtown was the place to be. But when Otto Woermke died in April 1981 — he was in the apartment upstairs from the restaurant, getting ready for another day of work — loyal customers wondered what would happen to the old place.

John and Mary Wright wondered, too. When they heard that Erne Woermke was selling the place, they strolled inside for a look.

"We both kind of like old buildings, and we thought we'd come in here," Mary Wright said. "It was out of curiosity, mainly."

But when the couple heard that someone was interested in buying the place, and that he wanted to tear out the old soda fountain to build a fancy Italian restaurant, curiosity turned to fear.

"I just couldn't bear to think of someone getting rid of that old soda fountain. I honestly got just possessed with it," Mary Wright said.

So they bought it. And today, more than a dozen years after the Wrights bought the place and 62 years after it first opened, the Old Mill Tasty Shop is pretty much the same place it used to be. That's the way the Wrights — and a whole lot of other people — like it.

Many people see John and Mary Wright as visionaries. After all, they were operating a restaurant in Wichita's historic warehouse district long before Old Town was the hot spot for restaurants and nightclubs.

"Yeah, I'm a pioneer," Mary Wright said. "It was too late in our century maybe to go out on the prairie and be prairie pioneers, so we came to the city and became urban pioneers.

"I am a person that, if I set out to do something, I generally do it."

Lunchtime at the Old Mill borders on frantic, with all the tables full and waitresses scurrying around like ants at a picnic. One particular waitress, Gale Cowan, is one of the best in town, and can rattle off the flavors of shakes and malts faster than you can say you're hungry. Behind the fountain is a genuine soda jerk, just like the old days.

People have met, courted and even married in the old eatery. The almost overwhelming sense of history in the original booths, walls and tin ceiling always amazes the Wrights. They respect history so much, in fact, that the menu still includes the Woermkes' famous chili, as well as their peanut butter and banana sandwich.

"I see this as a place that brings people together," Mary Wright said. "Every week a new story comes in the door, someone telling you about memories they have."

The part of the Old Mill that you don't see is the Wrights' farm outside Cheney. There, John grows tomatoes, lettuce, melons and other produce

Gale Cowan, a 10-year employee, shares a fun moment with Mary and John Wright.

SNAPSHOT BIOGRAPHY

Mary Wright was born March 14, 1948, in Salina. John Wright was born Feb. 22, 1947, in Wichita. They met when they were students at Wichita Southeast High School, and the couple married Feb. 22, 1965, in Kingman. They live outside of Cheney and have two children, Shannon and Don. Years in Kansas: John 45, Mary 44.

that Mary uses at the restaurant and in her catering business.

"We enjoy our time out here and our privacy," John Wright said. "I need to come into the city more often, though, I get a little wild out here."

He likes his garden, though, where he has grown a particularly tasty variety of melon. "See, there's the moon and the stars around it?" he said, turning over the ripe melon. "That's why it's called Moon-and-Stars."

And that's what John and Mary Wright reached for when they reopened the Old Mill Tasty Shop. It was their dream.

"When you come to the realization of your dreams, to see that coming true, well, it's worth anything you do," Mary Wright said.

Opposite: Mary and John Wright kept the Old Mill Tasty Shop pretty much the same place it used to be.

Quiet But Powerful

Grace Wu-Monnat helps others improve body and mind through t'ai chi

Wichita

Grace Wu-Monnat moves with the balance of a gymnast, the grace of a ballerina, the strength of a boxer, the speed of a hawk.

She is demonstrating the "supreme ultimate form," an ancient Chinese martial art known as t'ai chi, and her students watch with wonder and respect. Even in a sweaty downtown studio that Wu-Monnat shares with the Wichita Fencing Club, it is easy to see why she is a master.

"Feel like you're going down, without really dropping," she told the group of about a dozen students. Balancing her body on her right foot, she stretched her hands out in front of her and brought her left foot around to her side.

"Three . . . and don't lock the left knee, four. . . . Stay back a little. Travel, travel, take time, three. . . .

SNAPSHOT BIOGRAPHY

Grace X. Wu-Monnat was born Feb. 13, 1958, in Shanghai, China. She received her bachelor of arts in physical education from Shanghai Teachers University and a master's in sports administration from Wichita State University. She and her husband, Daniel, were married May 15, 1992, in Wichita. Years in Kansas: 9.

And pivot the left foot, pivot, pivot, four. Give enough time to use the muscles. Good."

It is with this same grace and balance that Wu-Monnat, a native of China and the granddaughter of one of that country's most famous martial artists, lives her life in America.

"I enjoy here now," she said, her accent an ever-present sign of her Chinese heritage. "When I first come, I have a kind of adjustment to make. Now I feel really comfortable."

She did make it, using her background in the martial arts and advanced degrees in physical education to open a martial arts school in Wichita. Wang's Wu Shu School is named for her maternal grandfather, Wang Zi Pin, who taught her the martial arts when she was very young.

"I think martial arts has the own beauty of it," she said. "I think showing the movement is its own beauty. I think it's important now to help the people coming to my school to become healthy and strong. And also it helps them become better person."

Recently, Wu-Monnat began holding weekly t'ai chi classes on the banks of the Arkansas River from late spring through early fall. Every Saturday at 8 a.m., anybody who wants to experience the tension-relieving benefits of t'ai chi can come and try it — free of charge.

"It's my kind of public service," she said. "It is open to the public. Sometimes we have a few people, sometimes more."

Whether on the riverbank or in her studio, she likes helping people discover the physical and mental balance the martial arts can bring.

"I do enjoy working with people. That's one of the first things about my profession. I say I want to be able to work with people.

"Here, with t'ai chi, they learn about balance. It's a softness, but also firmness. Moving, but also contained. It works the body and the mind," she said. "I think it helps people learn how to focus their own energies and learn about the balance in life."

Wu-Monnat balances her own life with another hobby — practicing traditional Chinese calligraphy and painting delicate watercolor pictures of nature. "It's helped me learn how to be calm."

That calmness, in turn, translates to her martial arts work and her teaching. She is quiet but firm, understated but inspiring. And her students love her. People travel from across the region to attend weekly or biweekly classes at Wang's Wu Shu School.

"That's it, Jim! Right there!" She stopped a student in the midst of his t'ai chi routine, then directed him to the right position as if she were helping someone hang a picture on the wall. "Push the back leg forward a little . . . straight up . . . no, forward. . . . Open up. That's it!"

The man's focused grimace melted into a faint smile, and Wu-Monnat continued her demonstration.

"Everybody's here for a different reason," she said. "But everybody learns what martial arts is about. It is quiet, but very powerful." Just like her.

Grace Wu-Monnat paints Chinese calligraphy in her home studio.

Grace Wu-Monnat leads a t'ai chi class on a summer Saturday morning in Riverside Park.